MINES, MINERS AND MINERALS

WESTERN NORTH CAROLINA'S MOUNTAIN EMPIRE

LOWELL PRESNELL

WORLDCOMM®
a division of Creativity, Inc.

Publisher: Ralph Roberts
Vice-President: Pat Roberts

Editors: Susan Parker, Julie Burns

Cover Design: Gayle Graham
Interior Design & Electronic Page Assembly: Susan Parker

10 9 8 7 6 5 4 3 2

Library of Congress Cataloging-in-Publication Data

Presnell, Lowell , 1941-
    Mines, miners, and minerals : western North Carolina mountain empire / Lowell Presnell.
        p.   cm. --
    Includes bibliographical references and index.
    ISBN 1-56664-135-7
        1. Mines and mineral resources--North Carolina--History.
    I. Title.
    TN24.N8P74   1998
    338.4'7622'09756--dc21   98-36574
                                                                        CIP

The author and publisher have made every effort in the preparation of this book to ensure the accuracy of the information. However, the information in this book is sold without warranty, either express or implied. Neither the author nor WorldComm® will be liable for any damages caused or alleged to be caused directly, indirectly, incidentally, or consequentially by the information in this book.

The opinions expressed in this book are solely those of the author and are not necessarily those of **WorldComm®**.

Trademarks: Names of products mentioned in this book known to be, or suspected of being trademarks or service marks are capitalized. The usage of a trademark or service mark in this book should not be regarded as affecting the validity of any trademark or service mark.

WorldComm®—a division of Creativity, Inc.—is a full–service publisher located at 65 Macedonia Road, Alexander NC 28701. Phone (828) 252–9515, Fax (828) 255–8719.

WorldComm® is distributed to the trade by **Alexander Books**™, 65 Macedonia Road, Alexander NC 28701. Phone (828) 252–9515, Fax (828) 255–8719. For orders only: 1-800-472-0438. Visa and MasterCard accepted.

This book is also available on the internet in the **Publishers CyberMall**™. Set your browser to http://www.abooks.com and enjoy the many fine values available there.

CONTENTS

Acknowledgements

Without the encouragement and assistance of Dorothy Hussey, a good friend and wonderful person, I would have never undertaken this endeavor. Being extremely literate, she knew there is very little recorded history of a people and industry that have been so important. Thanks, Dorothy.

Without the aid of local news, newspapers and other printed material, this would have been a most difficult task.

On the Cover: *The Chestnut Flat Mine*
Left to right: Ed Turbyfill, Arnold Blackburn, Claude Pitman, Rev. Jeff Willis, Merrit Sparks, John Duncan, Newland Sparks, Landon Pitman, Walter Buchanan, Ike Grindstaff, Roe Duncan, and Bob Duncan.

The author inspects remnants of the muck car
at Colberts Creek Balsam Mica Mine on August 23, 1997.

The small hole in the center is all that is left of an old mica
mine in Western North Carolina. Another 100 years, and
nothing will be left, not even a memory.

Introduction

Mining in Western North Carolina has played an important economic role in the lives of its people and the state's history, but there has been very little recorded about the industry, especially the day-to-day trials and triumphs of the individual miners.

The history books are filled with articles about frontier life, trade with Native Americans, railroad and road construction, the Civil War, mountain life and large mining operations but history has taken individual mines for granted. Most records that still exist are found in land or court records. These records hardly tell the story.

Some of the minerals that have been and still are being mined in Western North Carolina are alum, asbestos, barite, clay, columbite, corundum, copper, feldspar, granite, gold, garnet, graphite, gravel, iron, kyanite, lead, limestone, mica, marble, manganese, nickel, olivine, quartz, samarskite, sand, spodumene, tin, tungsten, talc, uranium, vermiculite, and many varieties of gemstones. Chromium, silver, tin, zinc, zircon, uranium and molybdenum have been mined on a lesser scale.

One of the questions that had to be answered when I decided to write **Mines, Miners and Minerals** was where to start. Early history of the area has been written about several times. All the printed material that survived probably has been expanded to its credible limit. The world at the time did not depend on our minerals, but the first settlers did. I also want to focus on the working miners and their families.

I will try to show why and how our Western North Carolina miners and mines have arrived at where they are today.

Lowell Presnell
September 1998

1

Early Explorers

The pursuit of gold and gemstones led de Soto and his Spanish army into Western North Carolina in the sixteenth century. Hopeful Spanish prospectors combed the mountains for the next one hundred and twenty-five years in the pursuit of the same.

After de Soto's mining in Western North Carolina, the next recorded mining[1] was in 1767 for clay, initiated by Thomas Griffiths. Griffiths was employed by Josiah Wedgwood, English manufacturer of fine pottery and producer of England's most prized chinaware. After testing a sample of the clay obtained from this area, Griffiths realized that it was vastly superior to the clay he was using. The clay came from a site in Macon County, then called the Joree Mountains, now called the Cowee Mountains near the Indian village Ayonee.

Griffiths traveled from Charleston with a group of men and equipment. He located the mine and purchased five tons of the precious clay from the Cherokee Indians. After mining the clay, it was loaded on pack horses and hauled from the mountains.

Once settlements to the east were reached, the clay was loaded onto wagons for the journey to the Charleston Port. When the clay reached England, the artist-manufacturer Josiah

---

[1]British Archives have the records.

Wedgwood used the Macon County clay in every piece of jasper; his finest product is a stoneware delicately colored with metallic stains while embossed designs remain white.[2]

The documentation of the Wedgwood Expedition is what makes it important and interesting, not necessarily the date. I have not found any written record but there is evidence to show that clay was mined before 1767. According to the natives, even the clay deposit at Ayonee had been mined by whites. There were white settlements scattered among the valleys and plateaus of the eastern slopes of the Blue Ridge Mountains. The great wagon road that extended from Pennsylvania into the Carolinas was already in place and well used. The large populations to the east would need the clay found in the mountains. All the pioneers' lives depended on what came from the earth, whether it came from harvesting game, farming it or mining it. Mining clay and talc to manufacture containers would have been common-place at the time, and the pioneers could have traded for these items. There were hoards of peddlers flocking to the mountains but steel and stone products would have cost a lot. Settlers did not have the hides to trade; besides, they were much harder to swindle than the trusting natives.

Henry Timberlake, early explorer to Western North Carolina, wrote of the wealth of products produced by the Cherokees and spoke of the beautiful gems in the possession of the Indians which were used in ceremonial rites. That was of minor economic importance but during the nineteenth century, the miners, mines and minerals of Western North Carolina would become large enough to have an economic impact not only on the region and state but the entire country.

---

[2]The record of this mining expedition exists in England and was printed in the *Asheville Citizen-Times* August 13, 1950, and October 20, 1956.

Early Mines

Native Americans and then Spaniards had mined for the mineral wealth of Western North Carolina for at least 300 years before modern mining began. Modern miners found that if they would dig in ancient mines, they would generally find a valuable mineral. Most ancient mines were destroyed this way.

Very little hard-rock mining was done by the ancients; the Horse Stomp Mine, located on Rich's Knob in Mitchell County, was an exception. Before the heading of the mine collapsed, it was explored by D.D. Collis before the turn of the century. The ancients carried the heading about 400 feet, turning slightly and going down for at least eighty feet. The entrance was dirt and had been cribbed with chestnut logs. There is no indication of what the miners were looking for. The mine dump consisted of Carolina gneiss, impure quartz and gossan. The absence of peacock pyrite, covellite or copper stains on the dump precluded copper as a possibility, so apparently it was gold. The quartz must have carried the mineral the ancients sought. The size of the mine indicated that it was a successful operation.

Most ancient miners only mined the topsoil. This was evident at the Sink Hole Mine, located near Bandana in Mitchell County. The workings of the mine resembled a large railway that extended about a third of a mile along the ridge and was sixty to eighty feet wide at the top. There was evidence that iron tools

The Sink Hole Mine in Mitchell County, a mecca for rock hounds, was first mined by the ancients for mica, then silver, then mica again.

had been used but only stone tools were found. Charles P. Stewart of Pineola excavated one of the old digs to a depth of forty-two feet. He found a section of a tree with 300 rings of growth. This was one of the means used to determine the last time a mine was active. The trees on the dumps and in the pits at the Hawk and Clarissa were cut and the growth rings counted. On one dump, a chestnut tree measured twelve feet in circumference three feet above ground.

Mound builders were believed to be the ancestors of the first American Indians who inhabited the Ohio and Mississippi River Valleys. It was a popular belief that mound builders were responsible for the ancient mines. Red-rum mica was found buried in their graves, but the graves were 600 years old and the mines only 300 years old.

During that period, the Catawba Indians held the land east of the Blue Ridge and the Cherokee Indians held the land to the west. The Toe River Valley was a mutual hunting and fighting ground but there were no large permanent villages.

It is believed that mica on display in a museum in Madrid came from the Sink Hole Mine. The Native Americans tell of white men on mules who came from the south and carried away a white metal. This points to the Spaniards. The author personally believes the Native Americans had an effective trade system. Spear points found are often made of stone not native to the area. There are so many, the natives must have traded for and used them.

It is also the author's belief that there were villages in the Toe River Valley over 600 years ago and they mined mica and traded it from coast to coast. The Spaniards came into the area about 1540 looking for gold and gems and knew that where the Indians had mined, there was probably something of value. This would explain some of the sites being over 300 years old. Some of the sites, such as the Horse Stomp in Mitchell County and the Ancient Mine on Bolens Creek, contained nothing of value that was visible. The soft, black rock found in the dump is hornblend schist common to that area. The old Ancient Mine on Bolens Creek has kyanite close by. The Spaniards could have confused this with blue sapphire.

When James Moore and Maurice Matthews visited Cherokee country, present-day Cherokee County, they reported that they were told of bearded white miners working twenty miles west of the Indian village at Peach Tree. The evidence of gold mining in Cherokee County about 400 years ago is unmistakable. The Cherokees say that the miners were there for three summers until they were killed by the natives.

In 1913, William R. Dockery of Marble explored a mine on the mountain east of the community of Tomatla with timbering apparently similar to that in the Horse Stomp Mine. A few years earlier, an old gentleman by the name of Palmer got directions from the Indians to a lead mine. A fellow by the name of Dockery and three of Palmer's sons searched for the mine. On the spot where the mine was supposed to be was a large forked chestnut tree. They cut the tree and dug out the stump. After removing some dirt a shaft was discovered that was an eight foot square, cribbed with oak beams at three foot intervals. The shaft was filled with water up to sixty-four feet. They could push an iron pipe another seventeen feet through water and talc mud. After that, Dockery found three other shafts in the area; one was in solid rock. A Spanish coin mold was found nearby. An old furnace of unknown origin was found but later destroyed when a house was constructed near the location. Unusual numbers of beads, bones and arrowheads were picked up on the ridge above the tunnels and shafts, indicating a location where the Indians and the Spaniards engaged in battle.[1]

[1]Muriel Early Sheppard, *Cabins in the Laurel* (University of North Carolina Press, Chapel Hill, N.C.), 1935.

Iron Mining

When the early settlers had scattered over the Piedmont and had commenced to settle the mountains, two kinds of iron were found: magnetite, hard and black, and limonite, a brown ore. The best ore contained over seventy percent metallic iron, and limonite yielded well over five percent metallic iron.

In 1750, Great Britain forbade the colonies to manufacture any iron product except pig and ore, but the imminence of war had a reverse effect—it stimulated, to a degree, the erection of iron works. The people of North Carolina had a few problems that had to be solved first. Money was foremost. They needed money to hire experts from the North and money to build and operate furnaces. Good people and equipment, as today, weren't cheap. However, records show there were two furnaces operating in Orange County by the end of 1770 and a prospect of another near Salisbury.

The large deposits of iron ore and exports from South Carolina led to the first iron works in Western North Carolina, the Buffington Iron Works at Kings Mountain. The starting date is uncertain but it was destroyed by the British in 1780.

The next serious iron mining in Western North Carolina was undertaken in about 1807, when Talbert built a forge to process this rich magnetic ore. In 1823, bar iron from Lincoln County Iron Works sold for $6.25 a pound and casting sold for five cents a pound.

By 1830, four iron works were in operation in Ashe County. Four others had been abandoned or destroyed by floods. Almost a hundred years later, those deposits were still being worked. Iron mining in Ashe County looked brighter than ever. Those rich deposits had gotten the attention of business people who were willing to invest their time and money.

One of those early companies and investors was Lansing Mining of Ashe County, incorporated June 28, 1918 to mine and process iron ore, build rail lines and switches, and operate steam-powered generators. The officers were George Cooke from Johnson City, Tennessee; C.S. Cooke and L.G. Boxwell from Nashville, Tennessee; and C.L. Park from Jefferson, North Carolina.

Hamilton Mining became a corporation at West Jefferson, North Carolina on April 7, 1919. The value of the stock was set at fifty thousand dollars. The officers were R.A. Hamilton and F.R. Shafer from Beaver Creek, Ashe County; G.L. Park from Jefferson; and H.F. Fries from Winston-Salem, North Carolina.

Ashe Mining formed a corporation on July 10, 1920 to build railroads and switches, operate steam-powered generators and mine and process iron ore. The officers were George W. Cooke from Johnson City, Tennessee; E.W. Stone and A.W. Cooke from Lunk Hammock, Pennsylvania; and C.L. Park from Jefferson, North Carolina.

When a site was chosen for an iron works, three key items were a must: iron ore, limestone, and coal or wood to fuel the furnaces. Western North Carolina has plenty of limestone and many of the deposits have been mined over the years, like the area near Hot Springs in Madison County.

These mines date back to the turn of the century. One of those companies, the G.C. Burgess Lime Company, incorporated June 18, 1912, mined several quarries and processed limestone on location. It has been suggested that Burgess primarily mined the limonite iron ore and refined it by using the mined lime as a flux. The company closed in 1917.

After limestone was no longer needed by the steel industry, new uses were discovered. Farmers used limestone to sweeten the soil so the crops would grow. One of the companies that provided agricultural lime was Clinchfield Limestone Company. That company mined the deposit at Woodlawn in McDowell County and then moved to Fletcher in Henderson County and incorporated on April 2, 1915. On December 29, 1925 they merged with Blue Ridge Lime. The former limestone (dolomite) deposit at Woodlawn is currently being worked by Explosive Supply for lime and gravel.

A few individuals became wealthy from the iron industry; most did not. The Cranberry Mine, which operated into the twentieth century, produced iron of high quality. Foster A. Sondley, in his *History of Buncombe County*, noted that during the Civil War a factory built in Asheville turned out three hundred rifles per month using Cranberry iron.

Railroads did not come to the Carolinas until the 1850s. Until that time, all iron produced and not used locally had to be shipped to Charleston by wagon, and roads were almost non-existent. This kept major investors out of North Carolina. North Carolina also did not have coal for fuel except for the Deep River deposit.[1]

There was a shortage of experts in the iron-making trade. North Carolina offered free land and no taxes for ten years to anyone who would produce fifteen tons of iron a year. In 1860, North Carolina had forty-nine iron works.[2]

[1]*North Carolina Historical Review*, October 1932.
[2]*Ibid.*

Cranberry Forge

The paper trail leading from the Cranberry Iron Mine and Forge is a long one. The first to record a claim on the magnetite deposit was Reubin White in about 1775. At that time, settlements west of the Catawba River were forbidden by the British. However, trappers and hunters paid little attention to the royal decree of the British. That was not what kept Reubin and others from mining this deposit; it was the remoteness of the area. In the fall of 1826, a fellow from Tennessee named Joshua Perkins located the deposit. Things had changed in the past fifty years. Joshua knew very little about mining and minerals, but he knew someone who did. He gathered up a load of samples and headed over to talk with John Dugger and John Asher, who were operating a mine and forge near the Watauga River. The news was good. After some tests, he was told the ore was high quality.

He also found out that a North Carolina law stated that anyone finding ore on vacant land could enter the land and build a tilt hammer forge. Whenever it was established that 5,000 pounds of wrought iron had been produced at the new forge, the state would grant a bounty of 3,000 acres to cover the site. This act had been passed by the 1778 General Assembly.

Joshua recognized the opportunity and wasted no time. On February 9, 1827, Joshua Perkins, along with his brothers, Ben and Jake, had their entry recorded in Raleigh, North Carolina. On the fourth Monday of October, 1829, they proved in the Burke County court that they had produced the 5,000 pounds of wrought iron required. The warrant of survey is dated February 2, 1830 and the grant was issued on December 10, 1833. The Perkins brothers were the first individuals to own the Cranberry Iron Mine and surrounding 3,000 acres of land. To produce the 5,000 pounds of wrought iron, the Perkins brothers had built a forge dam a mile below the deposit in 1828. Cranberry bushes had to be cleared from the site where the forge was built and this was how it got the name Cranberry Forge. Drilling and blasting in those days was not practical. It would not be required for another fifty years. A pick and shovel would work just fine. I have not figured out why hollowed-out logs were used for wagon beds. It seems to me that common rough hardwood lumber would have worked fine and was available in the area.

William Wiseman, one of my ancestors, built and operated the first lumber mill west of the Blue Ridge at Ingalls, not far from Cranberry. The ore was mined from the shallow open pit mine. It was placed in the hollowed-out logs on wagons and hauled to the mill.

The Perkins brothers did okay for awhile but they made some bad business decisions and ran up some huge debts they could not pay. The Morganton Court ordered the property sold to satisfy the debts. The mine continued to operate most of the time in spite of legal problems. It is my opinion that there were too many people involved. Each time an owner would retire or die he would simply leave his share to his heirs. No doubt this policy caused management problems.

The surface ore was depleted by 1882 and underground mining was commenced by Cranberry Iron and Coal Company. In 1915, this company was reorganized. The Wise family owned the majority of 9,347 shares of stock. In 1930, the large tract of property surrounding the mine was sold. Some of the miners who worked the Cranberry Iron Mine during the late 1800s were: William Phillips, William Taylor, Frank Greene, George Shell, John Smith, Charlie Gouge, Henry Richardson, Noah Maloane, William McGee, Benjamin Greene, Ambro Miller, John Callahan, Walter Callahan, William Tolley, Columbus Wilds, Broskey McKinney, James Tolley, Audie Gevin, Strawberry Phillips, James Thourpe, Landin McLin, James Freeman, William Runnion, Muncus Lewis, Johnson Buchanan,

Viva Buchanan, James Peterson, Elisha Briggs, Hardie Hunter, Burglow Stanton, Joseph Freeman, Frank Williams and Robert White. For each job in the mine, there were probably ten related jobs.

Iron forges need tremendous amounts of heat. Western North Carolina did not have the coal for fuel, but did have hardwood that was converted to charcoal and used for fuel. Producing charcoal was a major industry for Cranberry. In fact, at one time, there were no trees left in the area.

The iron produced at the mine in early years was hauled by wagon to many locations, including Asheville and Johnson City; during the Civil War most of it went to Camp Vance near Morganton. A better method of transportation was needed.

The first train arrived at Cranberry Forge on the thirty-four miles of newly placed narrow gauge tracks from Johnson City in 1882. The narrow-gauge line was not popular but the construction of a standard-gauge line was ruled out because of the much higher cost. The name of the line was East Tennessee and Western North Carolina. It was called the Tweetsie because of the sound of the whistle. Tweetsie was supposed to be used to haul iron ore, but once it was in place, it hauled almost everything, including mica, timber, lumber, bulk farm supplies and equipment. Eventually, this line extended to Boone with a total length of sixty-six miles. It was the longest narrow-gauge in the world.

Before the turn of the century, Cranberry would get its second railroad. The Camp brothers of Chicago laid track from Cranberry to Pineola. It was incorporated under the name of the Linville River Railway, but did not last long. It was primarily used to haul timber.

When the huge tracts of virgin timber were depleted, the Camp brothers moved on. The Linville River Railway became part of the East Tennessee and Western North Carolina system that extended to Boone. According to *History of Avery County* by Horton Cooper, Sherman Pippin of Roan Mountain was engineer on that line for forty-five years. The line closed from Cranberry to Boone in 1940 and from Cranberry to Elizabethton in 1946.

Gem Mecca

Western North Carolina counties became a mecca for gem seekers: Alexander County for emerald and hiddenite; McDowell and Rutherford for gold; Burke and Catawba for gold and garnet; Mitchell for emerald; Cleveland for emerald and gold; Yancey, Haywood, Jackson, Macon, Clay, Transylvania and Cherokee counties for rubies and sapphires. Most counties had semiprecious gems such as aquamarine, garnet, amethyst and kyanite.

The Asheville Democrat reported December 5, 1889:

> "Our friend G.D. Ray, Esquire of Yancey gave us a pleasant call Monday and showed us some beautiful jewels of Aquamarine which were as brilliant as diamonds. All these and many more of various kinds Mr. Ray has gathered in the splendid county of Yancey, which will yet prove one of the richest and most attractive counties in the state. All it lacks are railroad facilities to bring to light the valuable treasures which now lie dormant in her forest and in her soil. Mr. Ray says he can dig out chrome ore which will yield fifty percent of chrome oxide and exist in inexhaustible quantity and is easily taken out. Four hands got out one carload of ore in two days."

That deposit of chromite was located at Daybrook and was still being worked for olivine as of 1997, one hundred and eight years later. Apparently Mr. Ray loved to collect gemstones and had collected many over the years. Most of the gemstones in his collection had been cut from minerals discovered during his mining operations. After his death, this valuable gem collection was mistreated and the location of most of those gems are unknown today.

The *Asheville Democrat* article states that "iron, mica, kaolin and other valuable minerals and ores abound" and "The splendid timbers have long been noted," as well as "A railroad through the county will find plenty to do for a time in transporting raw materials to market. The *Democrat* sincerely trusts it will not be very long before one or more railroads will traverse that splendid old county."

The following article appeared in *The Asheville News*, October 23, 1869, titled "Western North Carolina, its advantages and inducements it offers to immigrants in climate, soil, production and healthfulness" by H.P. Catchell, M.D., Professor of Physiology and Principle of Medicine and editor of the Department of Climatology and Hygiene for *The United States Medical and Surgical Journal:*

> "Gold—this so greedily sought metal has long been mined in North Carolina and found in four of the western counties: Cherokee, Clay, Jackson and Yancey. Silver—this useful metal exists in Clay, Watauga and Yancey.
>
> "Several mines have been recently discovered in Watauga County. Copper—there are two well defined copper districts in which occur many large veins. One of these in Jackson County extends across the mountains into Macon and Haywood Counties. Another belt is found in Alleghany and Ashe Counties. In both these districts the veins are developed on a very large scale. Unlike most, if not all other copper mines in the country, they are found in hornblend slate.
>
> "Iron—one of the most valuable accumulations of iron in the country is found in this section which has long been famous for the fine quality of the metal which it yields.
>
> "The magnetic ore, so well adapted to the manufacture of steel, is found in Mitchell, Madison and Haywood Counties.
>
> "Another bed accompanies the limestone of Transylvania and ore of the most important and extensive deposits in the country crosses the entire breadth of Cherokee. It belongs to the variety of specular or hematite ore.
>
> "Chrome iron—this mineral is found in Yancey, Mitchell, Watauga and Jackson Counties.

"Graphite—this rare and valuable mineral is found in Macon and Jackson Counties."

We know the Spanish mined for gems in Western North Carolina. We do not know what they found because of their secrecy. We know Native Americans mined for gems because of their use in tribal ceremonies. But one of the first commercial minings of gemstones was undertaken by C.E. Jenkins in 1871, when he sank a shaft in search of rubies and sapphire at Corundum Hill in Macon County.

Buck Creek and the Behur Mine at Elf in Clay County were mined for rubies and sapphire at about the same time. Meminger and Hooker Mining Co. in 1890 was mining corundum at the mouth of Muskrat Branch in Clay County. Commercial removal of rubies from the alluvial gravel in the Cowee Valley area of Macon County started in 1895, and rhodolite garnet was mined for a short time in Macon County during the late 1800s. In the 1880s, rubies were mined by U.S. Hayes on Sampson Mountain at Bee Log in Yancey County. Small red rubies can still be found in the stream below the Hayes Ruby Mine.

Joseph Hyde Pratt stated in 1905 in *The Southland* that the American Gem and Pearl Company of New York was mining beryl in Mitchell County and the gem mining syndicate of St. Louis was mining rhodolite in Macon County. Pratt also mentioned mining for aquamarine in Mitchell County by Virginia-Carolina Gem Company of Shenandoah, Virginia in 1911. Pratt states that the Connely Amethyst Mine in Macon County had been worked by the American Gem and Pearl Company of New York, and Rhodes Amethyst Mine in Macon County had been worked by Passmore Gem Company of Boston.

The Wiseman Mine was owned by the author's great uncle, M.D. Wiseman, and his wife, Matilda. Records show M.D. had leased the mine out for several years before Pratt's writing in 1905 and had allowed individuals looking for gemstones to search for aquamarine in the topsoil. After M.D. Wiseman returned from the Civil War, there was a market for mica, so the location was mined some for that mineral. Before commercial mining for gemstones was commenced, the area was covered with pot holes or "ground hog holes."

The Hungerford Mine located at Grassy Creek, near Spruce Pine, was originally operated for mica; however, it produced such fine gem-quality aquamarine, it was purchased in 1894, and systematically worked for gemstones. It produced some of the best aquamarine gemstones in the world. After the Hungerford Mine closed, flawed golden beryl crystals remained in the muck and weeds. Also, more emerald crystals could be found at the closed Crabtree Emerald Mine because it was less accessible to visitors.

The Wiseman Mine, located in Mitchell County, was close by and, like the Hungerford Mine, has produced some of the best aquamarine gemstones ever found. The mine still produces today.

William E. Wiseman stands in front of his uncle Martin Wiseman's aquamarine mine, circa 1892.

Gold, Diamonds & Alum

During the late 1700s, there were rumors that the Spaniards were finding gold everywhere. Gold and silver seekers flocked to the mountains. Some of the precious metal was found, but the real gold rush did not come until around 1799, after twelve-year-old Conrad Reed found an interesting-looking seventeen pound "rock" on his father's farm in newly created Cabarrus County. This rock turned out to be a nugget of gold. After a couple of years his father, John, took it to town and came back with $3.50. Later, the mine was opened and produced nuggets up to twenty-eight pounds. Today, the mine is a tourist attraction.

New gold discoveries continued and mines opened in thirteen counties. Those in Burke and Rutherford were so rich that by 1825, these counties were the scenes of the nation's most extensive gold mining operations and gave North Carolina its early name, The Golden State.

Gold is a mineral familiar to everyone. Those who have it want more, those who do not have it would like some. Most people do not know that gold exists about everywhere you might look, but it is difficult to find. If you go walking on dirt, you probably are walking on gold. The reason most people have never found any is because it is so small. Most gold mined today is so small it cannot be seen with the naked eye. Modern recovery methods can recover it. Methods of recovery today are efficient enough to have kept the price for gold down. In fact, the price has dropped a little in the past few years. Do not run out and trade your gold for paper just yet. The recovery efficiency hasn't improved that much.

Records of gold mining east of the mountains have been kept, but records of gold mining in the mountains have not been kept. Gold has been mined in all our western counties. In Yancey County, the R.V. Edwards property was mined during the 1800s at Bee Log, and in 1929, some mining occurred on Bill Allen Branch.

Discovery and mining of gold also led to the discovery of another mineral, pure carbon, also known as diamond. During the early gold mining days, thirteen authentic diamonds were found. Most were found at Bridletown in Burke County. The largest was found at Dysartsville in McDowell County.

The discovery of gold in Western North Carolina caused thousands of people to move into the area. Many were plantation owners who brought along all their farmhands, including their slaves. In 1833, there were approximately 5,000 slaves mining in Burke County alone.[1]

Between January 1831 and February 1840, the Betchler Mint coined $2,241,850 in gold coins. During this time, it was estimated that in Burke County alone, over a thousand men were devoting their time to gold mining. It is estimated that by 1814, the gold mining industry had brought a capital investment into the state of $100,000,000.

The Philadelphia Mint minted $11,000 of North Carolina gold in 1814. During the extensive mining period, it minted $9,000,000 in North Carolina gold. The most gold shipped to the Philadelphia Mint for one year was $475,000 worth in 1833.

Gold was discovered at Egypt Township, according to *Bransons Business Directory* for 1868-1869. Between 1799 and 1860, it is estimated $50,000,000 to $65,000,000 in gold was mined in Western North Carolina.[2]

The fact is that most mining company records were destroyed. Individuals did not keep records. Gold dust and nuggets were used as a medium of exchange, and a lot was lost or kept secret. Filled orders were shipped to other countries and states directly from the

[1] Burke Historical Society, Heritage of Burke County, Morganton, N.C., 1981.
[2] *Asheville News*, Oct. 23, 1869.

mine. A close verifiable estimate as to how much gold was actually mined is not possible. One of the later and larger gold mining operations in the mountains appears to have been in Henderson County by Boilston Mining Company. There were some large mining companies in the region producing gold such as Fontana Copper but gold was not what they were primarily mining for. Boilston was mining the Boilston Creek, Forge Mountain area just for the gold and secondary minerals. Their mining operation lasted several years and involved a lot of money. When incorporated on September 25, 1880, the stock value was declared to be $100,000.

Something else of importance happened in Henderson County on September 25, 1880: Jonathan Williams, Albert Cannon and S.V. Pickens formed the French Broad Steam Boat Company. Their plan was to build steam boats and operate them between Brevard and Asheville. The author understands the company did not go under; in fact, just the opposite: they could not get off the ground. They did build at least one boat, but the river was too shallow; anyhow, that is another story.

Boilston Gold Mining Company must have been doing okay. According to legal documents on file at the Henderson County Court House, the officers declared on August 20, 1886 the value of the company had doubled to $200,000. Officers of Boilston all had local names: J.R. Jones, Matt Atkinson, G.M. Roberts, W.C. Jones, W.S. Harkins, J.E. Reid, W.W. Rollins, Morris Allison and W.G. Jones. The high price of gold has stimulated the industry, which is active in Rutherford and McDowell counties today. Lost gold or gold mines have always been hot gossip topics. The following story has made the circuit and probably is true.

In 1923, Dan Adams, a geologist from Western North Carolina, was contracted to purchase area mineral-rich land for the investment company of Crabtree Holdings, Inc. Dan hired a young fellow named Carter Hudgins from Marion, North Carolina to drive him around. Later Carter would become a well-known attorney. A particular parcel of property located on the headwaters of Crabtree Creek met the specifications and was placed at the head of their list. That location later became known as The Old #20 Mine (Carolina Minerals #20).

An old-timer by the name of Joe Ballew owned the property. Joe was said not to have trusted people and would not associate with others unless it was a must. Adams managed to contact him and after several meetings a deal was struck. The price was set at $1,500 and Joe would not accept anything except gold coins. There was a grassy bald not far from Joe's cabin. The exchange would take place there. He could not read or write and did not trust most people. He knew and trusted the postmaster at Little Switzerland. He would bring him along to read the document and count the money. When the gold arrived from Knoxville and at the designated time, Adams and Hudgins parked their car where the road ended and commenced to walk towards the clearing. Hudgins was carrying the heavy leather pouches when he ran headlong into a hornets nest. During the excitement, the pain and running, he forgot about the gold. When the bees were at last beat off, the gold had been lost somewhere in the woods. After a long search, it was found and they continued. Joe was skittish anyway, so they were afraid he would be gone. When they reached the clearing Joe was there waiting patiently. The gold, all in $20 pieces, was counted. He made his mark on the paper. It was a done deal. Joe pulled off his ragged coat and put the heavy gold in the sleeves. Joe left for his cabin, staying away from the trail.

No trace of the gold was ever found. After the government called in all the gold, someone paid Dr. McBee of Marion with a $20 gold coin. Some think that was one of the coins, but there is no proof. There is no evidence Joe put it in a bank or turned it in. People who knew Joe said he would have never turned his gold in for paper. After he died, his old cabin and grounds were searched by many.

Alum has also been mined in Western North Carolina. William Holland Thomas and his legions mined alum for medicine during the 1860s at Alum Cave, a place well-known by the Native Americans for its medicinal treasures. The mine was described not as a cave, but as a cliff overlooking a river in Western North Carolina.

Alum was used as an antidote to treat acute lead poisoning and to stop bleeding. It also will make pickles crisp and bread dough rise.

Early Economy

The gold-mine era that had provided the first real cash for the area had come and gone by 1884. The area could no longer function as a cash-free society. The Piedmont and coastal plains had land that was suited for growing tobacco and cotton. Western North Carolina did not have land that could be farmed to any extent, but it did have minerals. There was a market for these minerals and the demand was increasing daily.

The authorized visitors guide at the State Exposition in 1884 listed the state's mines by counties.

Iron: Alleghany 3, Ashe 4, Cherokee 6, Mitchell 2, Watauga 2 and Yancey 1.

Gold: Ashe 1, Burke 7, Caldwell 5, Clay 5, Cherokee 4, Jackson 3, Macon 11, McDowell 5, Polk 6, Rutherford 4, Watauga 2 and Yancey 1.

Copper: Alleghany 1, Ashe 8, Haywood 1, Jackson 9, Madison 1 and Watauga 3.

Mica: Ashe 2, Haywood 2, Jackson 3, Macon 4, Madison 1, Mitchell 11, Watauga 2 and Yancey 10.

A chart follows on the next page.

COUNTY	IRON	GOLD	COPPER	MICA
Alleghany	3	-	1	-
Ashe	4	1	8	2
Burke	-	7	-	-
Caldwell	-	5	-	-
Cherokee	6	4	-	-
Clay	-	5	-	-
Haywood	-	-	1	2
Jackson	-	3	9	3
Macon	-	11	-	4
Madison	-	-	1	1
McDowell	-	5	-	-
Mitchell	2	-	-	11
Polk	-	6	-	-
Rutherford	-	4	-	-
Watauga	2	2	3	2
Yancey	1	1	-	10

Figure 1: Western North Carolina's Productive Mines in 1884

When settlers moved west, they were constantly looking for gold and gems, but this had very little impact on the economy and was not of major importance to the early settlers. Clay, talc, building stone, grist mill grinding stone and iron would be more important.

Whenever tools and equipment were needed, the early settlers had to manufacture their own or hire a local craftsman to do it for them. Iron was available to fill this need. Those early forges must have been crude but they were everywhere. Manufacturing iron almost became a cottage industry. No record of iron-making in North Carolina from the early eighteenth century survives, although it is known that small quantities of pig iron were shipped to England in 1728, 1729 and 1734.

Hiddenite & Emerald

Hiddenite is known as the "Lithium Emerald." Lithium is the principal ingredient in spodumene. Hiddenite is the green gem variety of spodumene and is found nowhere else in the world except in Alexander County, North Carolina. We have no record of this mineral before the early 1870s. During that time, J.W. Warren owned a two hundred-acre farm just west of present day Hiddenite, close to where the cemetery is. While helping on the farm, his boys George W., Jeff, Hose, Alex, Bill and Pink would find odd-shaped green rocks. The boys weren't impressed or interested in keeping the ones they found, but their sisters, Katie and Sarah, were. They kept enough of them to get their father's attention.

J.W. Warren would bring crystals described as "green bolts" into a local business operated by Adlai Stevenson, the great-uncle of Senator Adlai Stevenson, during the early 1870s. This got the attention of a New York gemologist by the name of Dr. George Fredrick Kunz. At the time, Dr. Kunz was vice president of Tiffany's. Dr. Kunz previously had completed many studies of North Carolina minerals and published articles about those studies. He came back to North Carolina in 1874 and set up a mining operation in Alexander County in search of this rare mineral. Hiddenite had not been named yet and he did not find what he was looking for. However, he did find gem-quality emeralds, so the trip wasn't a total loss. Meanwhile, the merchant Stevenson was buying all of those so-called green bolts the farmers would bring to him. Dr. Kunz thought the mineral was diopside but it wasn't.

In this 1950s photo, the Southern Appalachian Mineral Society collects minerals at the Old 20 Mine located in Mitchell County.

In 1880 William Hidden, an acquaintance of Dr. Kunz, came to the area to help locate this mineral source. Dr. Kunz was very flustered with his efforts and had hired many people and searched many areas, looking for the mineral. The farmers did not seem to have any problem finding it and William Hidden had been there only a few weeks when his men found several pockets containing this mineral; the pockets also contained emeralds. Dr. Smith, working for the University of Kentucky, eventually identified the mineral as being a variety of spodumene. The mineral hiddenite was named after William Hidden, the person who submitted the samples for testing. It has been said that Dr. Kunz felt cheated out of the name because he was the one who had spent many years and lots of money looking for the mineral. Later a pink, purple variety of the mineral was found in California and was named Kunzite after the doctor of gemology.

William Hidden must have done okay for himself. The company he formed in 1881 was called the Emerald and Hiddenite

Mining Company. Hidden mined the area for several years before a land dispute closed him down. When the word got around about the find, William Hidden's company was not the only mining company there. Mining companies of all sizes came to the area in search of gemstones.

Many years later, on January 6, 1926, Burnham S. Colburn of Asheville leased a mine from J.E. Turner. Mr. Colburn wanted to locate some of this mineral, not because of its value as a gemstone but because of its rarity. Mr. Colburn was an avid rock hound who helped form one of the largest and oldest mineral clubs in the U. S., still active today after seventy years. It is named the Southern Appalachian Mineral Society (S.A.M.S.) and is the founder of the world-famous Colburn Gem and Mineral Museum in Asheville. During the period Colburn mined for hiddenite, his collection became the largest in the world. Through his generosity, museums all over the world display this rare mineral. In addition, one cut emerald from that same area was purchased by Tiffany's for one hundred thousand dollars.[1]

The Crabtree Emerald Mine in Mitchell County has probably been the most dependable and constant producer of excellent-quality emeralds in the United States. It was mined on and off from 1894 until the mid 1980s. Pat Aldridge of Marion told the author that he was working for Ted Ledford of Spruce Pine when the mine closed. Mr. Ledford hired Pat because his own health was failing and he already owned and managed Ledford's Gem and Mineral Shop. The mine was dormant for a few years but Mr. Ledford was convinced the mine had not played out. He hired Mr. Aldridge to pump the water out and search for emeralds. The pegmatite was still there but there were very few emeralds and they were small.

One day state safety inspectors showed up. The list of violations was long but could be corrected. Before long, federal safety inspectors came. Their list was too long. The cost would be too great. Pat Aldridge placed charges in the mine and blew out the pillars holding up the ceiling. These contained large amounts of emerald, so they were hauled away. The mine was closed. After

---

[1]*Mountain Mineral Monthly*, April 1992, article by Dorothy Hussey and corrections by Kemp Roll.

The entrance to the once-proud and famous
Crabtree Emerald Mine is now a rubbish heap.

the mine shaft was closed, surface mining continued and some emeralds are still being found.

Emerald is a variety of beryl with a trace amount of chromium. Aquamarine is the blue variety. Goshenite is pure beryl ($Be_3Si_6O_{18}$, beryllium aluminum silicate) and has no color. Heliodor has a trace of iron and has a gold color. There are others but that should be enough to tantalize your crystal, chemistry, geology and gemstone identification genes.

On May 7, 1857, an advertisement appeared in the *Asheville News* about the sale of 300,000 acres of land in Western North Carolina belonging to the estate of James R. Love. The strong selling point was: "valuable mineral discoveries have been made on many parts of the land and there is reason to believe they contain inexhaustible stores of valuable metals." If the owners had the ability to core drill this area or had known what the demand for minerals would be, the land would have brought a better price.

Up until 1763, Western North Carolina extended to the Pacific. Perhaps it was decided that there wasn't anything west of the Mississippi worth keeping. In 1789, all of the land west of the current boundary was given away. Some say only the best was kept.

Mica Mining

Mica was in demand by the pioneers to be used as window panes. Glass was available in large cities such as Charleston, but at first everything had to come to the mountains by pack animal. Window glass was hard to transport and expensive. There wasn't much mica east of the mountains, so some mica was traded or sold to merchants who would take it back to be sold and used as windows for houses or heaters.

When investors and manufacturers became aware of the remarkable properties of mica and the fact there was an abundance of it in Western North Carolina, they began to invent uses for it. Investors looked at the product and possibilities. They were convinced mica would be in great demand for a long period and invested at a rate that could be described as less than bullish, but they did invest. The industry was taking shape during the late 1850s but wasn't strong enough to continue during the war. During the late 1860s and through the 1870s, mica mining became more than a novelty. All the pegmatite districts of the area had some mining taking place during that period.

In 1858, mica from Jackson County was displayed at the South Carolina State Fair in Columbia by D.D. Davies. Some believe D.D. Davies was the first one to find a market for Western North Carolina mica. Could this mica have come from the Cox and Davies Mine? I suspect it did.

In 1883, half interest in the Clarissey Mine in Mitchell County sold for $10,000. In 1892, mica from the Ray Mine was displayed at Vienna during the World's Fair and was considered the best in the world. It was described as being a rich rum-colored mica.

By the turn of the century, gemstone mines were beginning to fill up with water and become overgrown with vegetation, but mica, feldspar and kaolin were pouring out of Western North Carolina. These minerals found their way into every house in the United States as scouring powder, china, pottery, glass, bathroom fixtures, wallpaper, automobile tires, roofing, electrical devices, plasters and paints.

As the demand for mica products grew, David T. Vance of Plumtree formed a partnership with his brother, T.B. Vance and H.R. Jones of Yumatilla, Florida to build a mica grinding plant and began operation in 1891.

Jake E. Burleson of Spruce Pine started opening mica mines in 1894. He eventually became the largest individual mica operator in the area, and went on to serve three terms as a North Carolina legislator. The Gibbs, Poll Hill, Birch, Cane Creek, Georges Fork, Henson Creek and River Mine at Penland were all operated by Burleson. Eventually, he owned mines from Georgia to Ashe County, North Carolina. During that period, the Gibbs and Poll Hill mines, located in Yancey County, produced over a half million dollars of high-grade sheet mica. At first he shipped mica by the wagonload ; after rail transportation became available, he built a mica house on top of Burleson Hill, near Spruce Pine, to grade and sheet the mica his mines produced. When the city of Cleveland, Ohio installed its first electric lights, J.E. Burleson personally delivered the mica used in those lights.

The Asheville Mica Company was founded in 1899. The president of the company was Vance Brown. The company invested heavily in the Toe River Valley. Brown owned 149,000 acres of land located between Three Mile and Cranberry that he inherited from his grandfather, Colonel Cathcraft. By 1904, he had opened a warehouse near the new railroad at Boonford. Before the railroad was operational in 1908, their mica was hauled by wagon to Marion. Gudger Fortner was put in charge of Brown's new warehouse at

This innocent-looking hole was a muscovite deposit that was mined to a depth of several hundred feet. Watch that first step—it's a long one.

Spruce Pine, built in 1910. In 1920, Asheville Mica bought the J.E. Burleson Mica Business. During that period, they had control of approximately seventy-five percent of the mica business in Yancey, Mitchell and Avery counties.

The Asheville Mica Company primarily bought and sold mica as it came out of the ground. By 1930, two mica houses in Spruce Pine were grading and cutting mica for the electrical industry. The mica plants supplying the electrical industry were Spruce Pine and Consolidated Mica Companies. At Plumtree, David Vance and family operated the Tar Heel Mica Company. They produced lampshades from sheet mica.

Spruce Pine Mica was founded in 1924 by Jake Burleson and Rastus Greene of Spruce Pine. Over the years, it ventured into almost all facets of the mica industry and it changed hands many times. During the early 1940s, Sidney Montague bought the Spruce Pine Mica Company. Today Spruce Pine Mica Company manufactures mica for the space industry and valves for respiratory equipment using mica from India. Richard Montague, son of Sidney Montague, is the company president.

As of 1997, the Vances still operate the Tar Heel Mica Company of Plumtree. They produce electrical washers from sheet mica imported from India, according to Don Vance.

Before 1900, the Vances in Avery County and J.E. Burleson in Mitchell County were providing industry with ground mica, first muscovite, then biotite. In 1906, Dr. Rouse of Pennsylvania was interested in mica and visited Spruce Pine. He purchased an excellent power site from Isaac English's son, Thomas A. English. When Dr. Rouse returned home to Pennsylvania, he worked with his broker, Robert R. Dent, to promote the company.

The English Mica Company was chartered in 1908. Robert Dent became so interested in the company he took charge. During that period of time, tires and tubes were made with natural rubber. When a tire was changed, a non-adhesive powder was used and most of the time it did not work. Raymond Dent, Robert's son, was changing a bicycle tire and found his powder can empty. There was a bag of ground mica from North Carolina available, so he used it. A year later he changed the tire again. The tube fell from the tire without sticking at all. Robert Dent, his father, was home this time and saw what happened. He took a hundred pounds to the Goodrich Rubber Company in Akron, Ohio. In a few weeks they wanted five bags, then a ton, then a car load. They used it in their vulcanizing ovens. This accidental use of ground mica in 1911 accounted for forty percent of the wet-ground mica industry by 1930.

There became many uses for ground mica; it would be hard to find and list them all. One use that caught my attention was implemented during World War II. Aircraft runways were critical and had to be built in the jungles and deserts, where there were no other roads. Building asphalt plants would have been a difficult, slow, time-consuming job. One central plant would be built and asphalt would be rolled out into thin strips and up into huge rolls. To prevent these rolls from becoming one huge glob, ground mica would be placed between the layers. When these rolls arrived at specific locations, they would be placed on machines called stamp lickers and rolled out, thus changing a surface that would not support the weight of heavy aircraft into one that would in a very short time.

Theo Johnson and brother-in-law Charles Gunter of Spruce Pine found a deposit of biotite mica schist between 1909 and 1911 on Judge S.A. Martin's property located in the Hanging Rock Valley. They did not have much luck in finding a market. They knew it would have to be ground when used and wore out several sausage grinders experimenting. They called their company the S.A. Martin Mica Company. Finally, in 1918, they got their first order for three tons.

Biotite was not mined anywhere else in the world except in a belt running south from the Big Bald to Altapass in Mitchell County. Robert Dent saw the future of biotite and decided to give it a try. In 1919, he bought out Johnson's share of the S.A. Martin Mica Company and changed from dry-ground mica to wet-ground mica. When Johnson sold out, he started promoting the Victor Mica Company, which developed the muscovite schist on Tempie Mountain, located east of Spruce Pine in Mitchell County.

The demand for mica continued to grow. The electronics industry probably would not be where it is today without mica. At one time, three-fourths of the mica produced in the world came from Western North Carolina. In 1954, mica was selling for about seventy-five dollars a pound. Only large sheets of mica were used at first. Around the turn of the century, the market opened for small mica. The old dumps were dug up and the mica removed.

During World War I, the demand for mica rose rapidly and Western North Carolina was willing, ready and able to meet the demand. As always, the miners of Western North Carolina lived up to the state motto "to be—not to seem." There was an abundance of this mineral and it had been mined since the first settlers had arrived. Over the years, the cost of labor remained low but North Carolinians needed jobs. Men would normally work the mine and women would grade and cut the mica.

Muriel Early Sheppard moved to Western North Carolina in 1928 with her husband, who was a mining engineer.[1] At that time mining was still extremely active, and she was fortunate enough to be able to interview people who were here during the beginning of commer-

---

[1]Muriel Sheppard, *Cabins in the Laurel* (University of North Carolina Press, Chapel Hill, N.C.), 1935.

cial mica, clay and feldspar mining. She had the good judgment to look up old records and stories before they were buried with time.

During 1858, North Carolina Senator Thomas Clingman was visiting Western North Carolina. While in North Carolina, he stayed overnight at Mr. Silver's home near Bakersville. The windows were made of sheets of clear isinglass. Senator Clingman wanted to know where the mica came from. He was shown the old dig. It wasn't long before he had a crew of men sinking a shaft. They found beautiful books of mica and feldspar glittering with pyrite. Crystals of mica were sometimes called books because they are made up of several thin, flexible sheets that separates easily at a point called the cleavage.

Clingman's crew found large books and plenty of muscovite mica. It was not the mica alone that got his attention. It looked as if there might be minerals that interested him more but more serious affairs required his attention. The operation was closed for a few years. It was the promise of silver that brought him back to the Sink Hole Mine in 1867. The ore was checked by experts and looked as if it was rich enough to bring up to $300 a ton. The Sink Hole was mined extensively but the ore never sold for over $3 a ton. The real value of the mine was yet to be discovered.

John G. Heap from New York, a tinsmith by trade, moved to Knoxville, Tennessee where he and longtime friend E.B. Clapp would eventually own and operate the Knoxville Stove Works. It is believed they not only built and sold stoves but owned a retail hardware store as part of that business.

What John Heap was doing in newly-formed Mitchell County in the early 1870s is not known by the author. While in Mitchell County, he located and took back with him mica from the Sink Hole Mine. The author can only speculate that he already knew about the mine and its mica. He had to know about mica's ability to stand heat. For whatever reason, the decision to use mica on a large scale would not only change their lives but would change the lives of many. The Knoxville Stove Works began to use the mica to manufacture windows in their stoves. Shortly thereafter, Mr. Heap, along with E.B. Clapp, returned to Western North Carolina and formed the Pioneer Mining Company of Heap and Clapp. They mined the Sink

Hole with great success. The shafts eventually expanded to between two and three thousand feet. The Sink Hole was worked
until the 1960s and today is a mecca for rock hounds.

As the demand for mica grew, Heap and Clapp leased wide tracts
of land. Others, such as Thomas Greene, were inspired to open mica
mines. Mr. Greene discovered the Cloudland deposit in 1870, but
previously mica was considered only a curiosity. Encouraged by the
success of Heap and Clapp, Thomas Greene opened the Cloudland
Mine. The first book of mica he found was eight inches by twenty-
four inches. It sold for $67, and would have sold for $250 if it had not
been weathered. It produced $4,000 in two months. The Cloudland
Mine was named that because most of the time its location high on
Mt. Pezzle near Hawk was covered with a thick layer of fog.

Later the mine was worked by Abernathy and Rorison and also
Heap and Clapp. Colonel Joseph K. Irby, an investor and mining
pioneer, estimated that by 1896 the Cloudland had produced
$100,000 worth of mica.

Some of the other Heap and Clapp mines were the Hawk Mine
(Cane Creek), which produced clear mica sheets that measured up
to eighteen inches by twenty-two inches. By 1896, it had produced
$75,000 worth of mica. The Clarissa Mine on Cane Creek had
produced $175,000.

As of 1935, the Clapp estate was still one of the largest holders
of mineral lands in the district.[2] It was estimated that the bulk of
the 400,000 pounds of mica mined in North Carolina from 1868
to 1882 came from Heap and Clapp properties. Most sold from $2
to $11 a pound.

Ella Clapp Thompson, daughter of E.B. and Alice Clapp, became
an attorney. She lived in New York and looked after the family estate
until her death in Mitchell County in 1945.

Much has been recorded about these true pioneers of the mica
mining industry. History has been recorded and can be located by
interested persons. I would like to share the story about Clapp's
death, which is not widely known. When the Clapps moved from
Tennessee, they made their new home on Snow Creek in newly

---

[2]Department of Interior Bulletin No. 740, 1935.

formed Mitchell County. One cold winter day, Elisah had a business meeting in Marion. When he left home the weather was threatening. With a little luck it would hold until his return.

The meeting lasted until late afternoon. The ride was a long one up through Turkey Cove and across the crest of the Blue Ridge. The rain had started to fall. A cold north wind had dropped the temperature and the rain turned to ice where it fell. When Elisah reached home it was late night and he was frozen in the saddle. The family helped him into the house where he thawed. By morning it was thought he would be all right. Pneumonia followed and lingered. This was in the early 1870s. Walking pneumonia was serious. The doctor suggested he take some time off, go to a place that was dry and warm. Elisah had little choice but to go. He let his plans be known that he would return to Snow Creek after recovery. He and his family moved to California. The pneumonia had severely damaged Elisah's health. His body would not heal. Snow Creek would never be his home again. Elisah Bogue Clapp, born at Amherst, Massachusetts in 1835, died at Los Angeles, California on January 18, 1874. The family had his remains buried in California. Joseph Irby was the administrator of the Clapp estate; J.L. Rorison bought the mica remaining in the estate and John Heap purchased the majority of the Clapp business property.[3]

An article appeared in a Knoxville newspaper about a visit to one of the Heap and Clapp mines (evidently the Cloudland from its location on Mt. Pezzle), by Dr. Hunt, Colonel Killenbrew and the author of the article. The title of the article was "Our Switzerland," Bakersville, September 14, 1877.[4]

A fellow by the name of Tom Jones was the hack driver. Apparently he did not spare the mules. Eventually the tongue broke off the hack.[5] In spite of Dr. Hunt's obesity, he was constantly jumping off the wagon to inspect a specimen of granite, gneiss, quartz, steatite or some other mineral which he spotted while riding along. He thought the country was filled with geological specimens calculated to run a scientist crazy. When at last they reached the mine, the sun was hot and bright. All the hues of the rainbow were reflected from

---

[3] *Roan Mountain Republican*, Oct. 7, 1876.

[4] Muriel Sheppard, *Cabins in the Laurel* (University of North Carolina Press, Chapel Hill, N.C.), 1935.

[5] A wagon for hire, primarily used to transport passengers a short distance (a taxi).

the minerals in the mine dump. It was difficult to divest the imagination of the fact that it was not gems that looked so enchanting. The visitors to the mine collected all the minerals they could haul, including a large valuable garnet given to them by a country man. The author felt the concluding negotiations for the day's transportation was worth noting.

"Tom, what do you get for your hack?"

"One dollar a day."

"Why, that is the cheapest riding I ever did. One dollar a day! Well!"

"Maybe, stranger, you don't understand. My hack gets a dollar a day, my mule gets a dollar a day and I get a dollar a day."

The mica vein of the Cloudland Mine was from six inches to three feet wide. Books from that mine eighteen inches by twenty-four inches were not uncommon. The mica was taken to a grading house where a chisel would be used to split them to the desired thickness. One book sold for $2,000. Apparently Indians had worked the mine in the past. Stone tools were often found.

The author of the article wrote that Mr. Heap had some fifteen to twenty separate mines and was constantly supplying stove manufacturers, lamp makers, etc. The refuse was sold occasionally to the makers of dynamite and they used it to blow up the rocks in the mines. The mica was ground into a coarse powder, soaked in a solution of nitric acid and sulfuric acid, and then dried. It could only be exploded by concussion; its power was enormous. Later a good market for scrap (powdered) mica would be found, but until that happened the scrap would have to be disposed of by whatever means was at hand.

There was no limit to how thin you could split the mica sheets. You may split as long as you could see it and with a microscope you could split it until it disappeared. In the late 1800s, North Carolina and the United States began to realize the magnitude of the wealth located in the pegmatites of North Carolina's western counties. Up until that time this national treasure had been largely taken for granted and treated with little importance.

The United States Geological Survey in 1893 dispatched Arthur Keith to Mitchell, Avery and Yancey counties to commence map-making of the Spruce Pine pegmatite district. This was a tremendous undertaking and continued for several years by several groups.

In 1923, D.B. Sterett made substantial progress. Over the years, North Carolina Geological and Economical Survey and also the United States Bureau of Mines continued the effort. During the 1940s, some nineteen geologists and associates were working the area. By 1948, maps had been published showing thirty-one square miles of the Spruce Pine pegmatite district.

At this point, the author speculates that the state still was not too interested. The hard-working miners of Western North Carolina could have put these pegmatites on the Capitol lawn faster than that. Located within this thirty-one square miles were 450 pegmatites; of these, 280 had certain economic value.

Zack McHone of Mitchell County believed he was the first man to sell a book of mica from that county. Zack had heard that you could sell mica in McDowell County. The problem was he did not know that isinglass and mica were the same mineral. He had dug up isinglass as a child while building a playhouse for his little sister. He went back to the site and dug up a huge book of mica. He did not know just how it should be prepared for market. He figured at least it should be nice and square. After awhile and two hand saws, he carried the mica to Marion and got $7.75 for it in about 1870.

The slump in the economy of the 1870s left the mountains with plenty of minerals but little cash to mine and market them. The state and federal governments were not going to help the people because so many had straddled the fence during the war. Investors and manufacturers from other areas had the means and knew how to develop and market those minerals. They also knew to control the market you had to control the supply. Many people came to the area and purchased or leased the mineral rights on as much property as possible. Two of those businessmen were L.B. Abernathy and J.L. Rorison. During 1891 and 1892, they leased hundreds of tracts of land that contained saleable minerals. They were not the only ones. What they did was good for the economy and welcomed.

Isaac English of Spruce Pine had always had an interest in

minerals. During the war, he met a Union Colonel by the name of J.M. Gere. Gere came to visit English after the Civil War. They came to talk naturally about mineral wealth of the mountains. English showed Gere a sample of mica and although he had no market for it, he knew where it was located. J.G. Heap and E.B. Clapp were already selling it. Colonel Gere was interested and a market was found. The Gere and English Mica Company of Spruce Pine was formed.

Hard currency was rare in the mountains. Most people either grew, manufactured or bartered for what they needed. Mica could be sold for instant cash. The rush for mica was on; it seemed every man able to use a shovel was out looking for it.

Up until now land had been sold without much regard to the actual boundary line. The courts were filled with lawsuits. Sometimes blood was shed. The most sensational killing in the history of the district, in 1885, was over the property on which the Cebe Miller Mine was located, between Spruce Pine and Bakersville. It was providing up to two tons of mica a day. Ed Ray and W.A. Anderson, sons-in-law of Judge Bowman of Bakersville, pulled some old land records. They saw a way they might get control of the mine, if not permanently, long enough to deplete its wealth by working it night and day. Cebe Miller owned the mine and had a crew working it. Miller refused to be scared out. Three men lost their lives and Judge Bowman almost lost his. Judge Bowman's advice was believed to be responsible for Ray and Anderson's claims. The lives were lost for nothing. The rich mica vein soon played out.

The Roan Mountain Republican ran an ad on Oct. 7, 1876, which said that "J.K. Irby, as administrator of E.B. Clapp, deceased, sold mica advertised in this paper to J.L. Rorison for $1,200."

The Asheville Citizen reported on March 10, 1887 that "Captain J.M. Gudger returned from Yancey County last Saturday and relayed that very little mica is being dug now, but still commands satisfactory prices. In addition, he relayed that the citizens of Yancey County inquire of every visitor, 'when is the railroad coming?' Every man, woman and child is interested in the expansion of the railroad from Asheville."

Many minerals had been mined from the mountains before

World War I, but for most of them the market was not strong. The mountain economy and demand for the local minerals had developed very slowly as the world, for the most part, did not know about the wealth of minerals to be mined from Western North Carolina. Mountain people were trained to live simply, work hard and waste nothing. The war changed that somewhat. World War I was the first war where a substantial number of meaningful, lasting jobs were created. New uses and markets were found for Western North Carolina minerals. Times weren't that good but most people did get enough of a glimpse of the good life to want to see more. That spirit carried over into the 1920s. It was unknown what the 1930s had to offer. One of the larger mica mines of 1920s was the Gibbs Mine of Yancey County. The mica color was rich rum. Books weighing up to two hundred pounds were mined.

Up until World War II, lower quality mica was sold to the electrical industry. Letterman Mines in Yancey County, consisting of two mines, produced large quantities of small mica best suited for the electrical industry.

My name being Presnell, naturally whenever I came across information about the Presnell Mica Mine located near Newdale, I was more than just a little interested. My ancestors were miners. They lived in the area at the time, so I sort of expected a familiar name to pop up. Each time I talk to a retired miner or locate written matter, some information normally does surface. I learned that the Presnell Mine was first worked for mica in 1872 by Amos Presnell and Dave Glenn. Whether or not that Amos was my great grandfather, I do not know and perhaps I never will. This does tell me something about the mine, though. This was near the beginning of commercial mica mining.

The Ray and Sink Hole Mines were also being worked in their infancy. Only large, clear mica sheets could be sold, so the Presnell must have been one of the better mines. Other operators of the Presnell were Gould, Watson, Carl and George Presnell, Lynn Carpenter, Sam and Ben Blalock. During 1942 and 1943, Meyers and Brown of New York operated the mine. At one time, J.L. Rorison leased this mine, along with dozens of other mines.

One of the last mica-producing mines on the South Toe River in Yancey County was the Carson Rock. This mine is located in the deep rock curve just north of the Mount Mitchell Golf Course on Highway 80 South, next to the swinging bridge across South Toe River. Harris Gibbs was still working this mine in the mid-1950s and it was producing plentiful large books of muscovite, but the quality was not extremely high. The mine is filled with water now.

Robert Tipton, a native of South Toe, told me he visited the mine while it was active. The entrance is in the rock wall on the east side of the highway. Once you enter, a shaft leads at a slight incline east up the ridge for several hundred feet. Another shaft leads west on a steep incline under the road and river. I do not know if the mine played out or the price of mica dropped, making this mine unprofitable. The quality of mica from the mine was low because it was stained with graphite.

I knew Robert's grandfather, Monroe Phillips, who also mined for a living. Monroe was a loner and kept the location of his mine a secret. He liked to mine where he had to walk in and out. Robert said he would see his grandfather leave before daylight, carrying a lantern and equipment, and return after dark.

The mine was located somewhere under the Black Brothers. Apparently, it was at least a good one-man operation mine and the mica quality was good.

The Sawnee Ridge Mine was located near Hamrick in Yancey County. Monroe Phillips worked that mine and got books of mica out that weighed several pounds each. Sawnee Ridge is located between South Toe River and Middle Creek. The mine itself was located on the east slope not far from where the old suspended bridge was located. Toward the end, Robert would go with Monroe to Spruce Pine and sell the mica, most of which would sell for $70 a pound or better.

A lone miner with low overhead could do quite well. At the time, miners were expected to earn a good living. For the most part, they were a trusted group and those that were not were soon weeded out. For most miners, credit from local merchants was not a problem. Old records show this to be true. When J.M. Jimmerson's Dry Goods closed in 1892, Mount Mitchell Mining

Company was on their books for $750. The debt was paid when the estate was settled.

There were mica mines operated in all Western North Carolina counties well before the peak of price and demand. The peak came in the early 1940s and ended in the mid-1950s. During this period, the government placed mica on the strategic minerals list and supported the price.

When the farmers laid by their crops, they would go to their own private dig and would remove the mica by the sackful. It does not seem reasonable that someone going out occasionally and mining a little mica could make a difference in the area economy. One person would not, but we aren't talking about just one person. Many people did this over a broad area and it was not just a pastime. Those people were serious. They depended on part-time mining to supplement their income. This provided much-needed cash and definitely influenced Western North Carolina's economy. These people would keep the location of their private digs secret, so they were never recorded.

In the early part of the twentieth century, mica was used in a variety of forms. Forms of mica include sheet, dimension, punch, wet- and dry-ground. In contrast to spar mines, most mica mines were underground.

During the first quarter of the century, the demand for smaller pieces of mica increased. Mica was beginning to be used in the manufacture of electrical parts and appliances, paint, wallpaper, roofing, decorative plaster, rubber, artificial Christmas snow and lubricants. Before the first big war, it had been used in the construction of windows for home and stove use.

In the 1920s there were primarily three mica corporations in Western North Carolina: The Spruce Pine Mica Company, The Consolidated Mica Company of Spruce Pine and the larger Asheville Mica Company, located at Biltmore. The Consolidated and Asheville Mica Companies mined practically no mica, if any.

During the 1930s, most large mining operations were on hold. There were seventy-five to one hundred small mines in the area being worked on an intermittent basis. The native mountaineer knew the area and mining methods and could produce the mica cheaper than the mining companies could—so cheap, in fact, that their labor wasn't even considered as an expense in earlier years. There was also a steady supply of mica from the large feldspar mining companies. The Spruce Pine Mica Company mined the Fanny Gouge Mine. In 1929, it was at a depth of over seven hundred feet and still producing mica and a rich soda spar.

Wet-ground mica was the highest-priced ground mica offered by the English Mica Company of Spruce Pine. The Biotite Mica Company of Spruce Pine also produced a wet-ground mica. Practically all of its mica was used in the rubber tire industry.

Dry-ground mica was offered by the Asheville Mica Company. The Victor Mining Company of Spruce Pine also operated a dry ground plant and sold almost all its product to the roofing industry.

The mica from the kaolin clay industry was called reclaimed mica. This material was mined by hydraulic methods along with clay. There were five plants in the Spruce Pine area processing this mica.[6] Three were operated by General Mica Company at Penland and two by Harris Clay at Spruce Pine. This mica was used by the roofing industry.

The Spruce Pine region was the most important ground-mica producing area of those times, including several mills near Franklin and one at Plumtree.

Western North Carolina was producing over half the mica in the United States during the 1920s. During World War II, Western North Carolina produced three-fourths of all mica produced in the world. Up until World War II, imports kept the price low.

Since the arrival of the first settlers, mica mining in Western North Carolina has never ceased. During the Depression, the demand for mica dropped drastically. Most miners returned to farming or logging. Some went to Henderson, North Carolina to work in the tungsten mines. There was also a good demand for moonshine whiskey. Though illegal, the profit was good and many turned to that trade. The industry thrived in the mountains until the price of sugar all but closed it down in the mid-1960s.

---

[6]A complete description of General Mica Plant Number 3 appeared in the September 11, 1929 issue of *Pit and Quarry.*

The onset of World War II renewed the mining industry. Mica mines that had managed to remain active retooled, hired more help and commenced to do what they did best—supply the world with high-quality mica. Shut-down mines were reopened and prospectors searched for new ones.

The price of mica went up drastically. Good mica was no longer used in roofing shingles and wallpaper. Additional plants were required to process the mica. Mines with adequate output operated their own grading and cutting houses. When the price support was removed in the late 1950s, the miners were getting about $74 per pound for their good-grade mica. There were reports that some mica brought $90 per pound. Today, mica has fallen on hard times again. It is sold by the ton instead of the pound. When looking at today's list of uses, one gets the feeling that it could easily become history. But history has shown that mica has always come back stronger than ever. When one looks at the quantity of mica left in mines, the quality of people working at North Carolina State University Mineral Research Laboratory in Asheville, the fine quality of our engineers, geologists and scientists, it might be wrong to mark mica off as history.

Vermiculite is a mica that is mined today and used as a lubricant and for buoyancy in oil-well drilling. It is also used in paints and roofing shingles. It makes excellent insulation and is used as potted plant soil. Spruce Pine Mica, Aspect Minerals, Warner Corporation and Franklin Minerals are major suppliers of this product today.

Mica mines have often been referred to as "ground hog holes" by people with no mining knowledge. There was no need to have huge open pits such as coal, copper, iron, phosphate, etc. had. There were a few open-pit mica mines, such as the one used for the mining of Lower and Browns Creek at Celo. Mines such as this one were hydraulically mined with large water cannons. Those mines were called jig mines. This method was used very little and these mines were the first to close because of the total destruction of nearby streams. Using this method, only small mica, along with clay, was recovered from pegmatite where the spar had altered to kaolin. Most mica mines were shafts. If you picture a mica mine in your head, you probably would think of a nice large square opening in the side of a mountain with a well-maintained road leading to it. It just wasn't that way.

Mica was always found with quartz. The quartz vein would normally not be over a couple of feet thick and that would be all the material that would need to be removed except for the extra that would be removed to make room to work. If the mica was in a pegmatite and the spar was also being mined, then the shaft could be huge, not remotely resembling a ground hog hole. Sometimes the vein would cross another, and if both contained mica, both would be mined. Sometimes the vein would just stop or change directions. All the material removed had to be loaded by hand and this was hard, slow work. Only the material that had to be removed was mined.

Mica miners weren't particularly interested in gemstones, but if an exceptional crystal of a gem mineral such as aquamarine was spotted, they would pick it up. Aquamarine was found in many of the pegmatite dikes that were mined in the area. It is blue-colored and a member of the beryl family. The composition is primarily beryllium, aluminum and silicate. It also could contain other minerals such as sodium, lithium or cesium. Pure beryl is called goshenite and has no color. Most non-metallic minerals, when pure, have no color but if a foreign atom structure is close enough sometimes, it will be accepted by the host atom. This can cause the mineral to have color and, depending on the atom, can determine what color. Emerald is beryl with a trace of copper. Golden beryl (helidor) gets its color from iron. Sometimes the mineral that caused the color change cannot be determined because of the small quantity.

Mica is normally found in pegmatites and pegmatites are one of the best places on earth to find many rare minerals. Some did not, but most mica miners passed up a great opportunity to collect those rare minerals and gemstones.

Feldspar

The first commercially mined feldspar in Western North Carolina was used as a cleaning powder. But, like mica, more and more uses were found for it, such as ceramics for the electrical industry, cookware, gemstones and quartz. Added to graphite, feldspar gives pencil lead its hardness.

At first, the pegmatites were mined for mica. The feldspar was discarded as waste, but later a use was found for it. The dumps were dug up and the spar removed. The spar had to be cleaned, especially of any black mineral, before it could be sold. Removal of impurities was called cobbing.

The companies with grinding plants would hire people to do this. These jobs were filled by cash-poor farmers and unemployed miners. A lot of people would cobb the spar and sell it by the ton. This way they could work at their own speed. During the big Depression, almost everyone needed a job and some spar was selling. Just about every mine dump was covered with cobbers.

The Ray Mines had been mined for mica for more than fifty years. There was a large area covered with a thick layer of feldspar. The Ray Mine dump was steep. The workers were assigned a particular area to work and occasionally someone's pile of spar or muck would break loose and tumble down the hill through other claims. A free-for-all would erupt, but after awhile they would shake hands and go back to work. The cobbers would haul the spar out by sled. When they had a load, they would haul it by truck or wagon to Micaville or Spruce Pine.

There were large mining operations in Western North Carolina but a large portion of minerals were mined by small two- or three-man operations. This mining usually took place on small private claims or after the larger mines played out. Individual miners would move in and remove what was left in the mines and dumps.

The first feldspar was mined in North Carolina and shipped to England in 1744. The first grinding plant was built at the Toll Gate Mine in Connecticut about 1850. The grinding stones were oxen-powered.

Most early feldspar mines were actually part-time mines. Only after the crop was in and enough food stored to assure winter survival would the farmer turn to mining. He would hook the horses, mules or oxen to the wagon (a.k.a. family transportation), sometimes take his wife to help, and head out to the old mica mine. There they would cob a load of spar from the dump. After it was cleaned and loaded, they would stop at the weight scales placed at the railroad yard. After the wagon was weighed, it would be unloaded and the spar inspected. If everything was okay, the rig would be weighed out.

The feldspar agent would pay cash on the spot and this was one of the few ways mountain people could get it. By the time feldspar was being bought, the average family did need cash. The barter system was no longer what it had been. It was not long before wagonloads of feldspar were coming from every direction. The Chesnut Flat and Sugar Tree Cove feldspar mines were first mined in about 1913.

Many farmers put down their hoe and plow and picked up the shovel and hammer to become professional miners. Between 1932 and 1940, most of the independent spar miners were replaced by large organizations.

The first feldspar-grinding plant in the area was called Pebble Mills. Small quartz pebbles from Pee Dee River were used in the grinding process. Soon the industry switched to metal rollers. No metal could be left in the finished product. Large magnetic devices were used to remove the tramp iron.

Even though there was commercial use for feldspar in the late nineteenth century, the industry did not excel until about 1911, when the North State Feldspar Corporation and the Feldspar Milling Company built plants at Micaville.[1]

During the early days of gem and mica mining, thousands of tons of feldspar were discarded as waste. In 1911, a carload was hand-picked and dusted. It was transported by oxen from Flat Rock Mine to the railroad at Penland and shipped.

W.E. Dibble of Petersburg, Virginia owned the Deer Park No. 1 Mine, where J.C. Pitman was job foreman. The first commercial load of feldspar from that mine was shipped from the Penland station in 1912. Also shipped from the Penland station a few years later were several carloads of spar from the nearby Chesnut Flat Mine, which was used to manufacture the Palomar Mountain Telescope.

In 1912 Theo Johnson and Charles Gunter sold a carload of feldspar to T.A. English and W.E. Blood for $2.60 a ton after it had been cleaned and sorted. It was removed from the Water Hole Mine in Avery County and shipped from Spruce Pine.

The demand for feldspar by pottery, tile and glass manufacturers was great. Just a few years earlier, feldspar was worthless. Now mines were being opened just for the feldspar. Mica was sold as a secondary mineral. At first feldspar was shipped from Western North Carolina to the Clinchfield Products Grinding Plant located at Erwin, Tennessee, the first of its kind in the south. D.J. Grayson, a native of Pennsylvania, was the original plant superintendent. The coarsest grind was ninety mesh, the finest was one hundred and forty mesh. Today, the grind is normally much finer.[2]

Soon the Clinchfield Plant had some competitors: the Erwin Feldspar Company at Erwin and the Tennessee Mineral Products Company, located at Bristol. All were getting their crude feldspar from Western North Carolina. Tennessee Mineral Products Company opened mines in Western North Carolina and started mining in 1921. At first, they mined the Wiseman Property on Beaver Creek. In October of 1921, they bought the lease from Martin and Carter of the Blue Ridge Mining Company for the Deer Park Mines. These mines were originally worked by the Dibble Mining Company. In 1931, the Spruce Pine district produced 103,200 tons of feldspar.

---

[1]Teacher training class of Burnsville, 1930.

[2] Ninety mesh is 1/90 of an inch. One hundred and forty mesh is 1/140 of an inch.

This was during a period when most industry, including feldspar, was in a state of decline.

In 1928, crude feldspar production for the United States was 210,811 tons. Western North Carolina provided 105,560 tons. New Hampshire was second with 30,343 tons. Prior to that time, Tennessee was the major producer.

In 1927, North Carolina ranked fourth but in 1928, North Carolina outranked Tennessee, New York and Maine. In 1928, New York ground eighty-four per cent of feldspar imported.

By 1929, there were five feldspar milling companies in Mitchell and Yancey Counties: North State at Micaville, Tennessee Mineral at Spruce Pine, Golding and Sons at Spruce Pine, Feldspar Milling at Micaville and Southern Feldspar at Toe Cane.

The North State Feldspar Corporation was shipping over 2,000 tons per month. The initial plan was to build a processing plant next to the Black Mountain Railroad and buy the spar from local miners. Lack of operating capital and bad weather soon overwhelmed the suppliers. The factories had to have a clean, high quality, dependable supply and to ensure this, they purchased property and mineral rights and operated company-owned mines.

The Goug Rock, which was one of the important North State Mines, was located on the east side of South Toe. On the west side of South Toe was the Black Mountain Railroad. The Goug Rock Mine was a shaft mine but most feldspar mines were, as they are today, open pits.

When the spar was hoisted out of the shaft, it was dumped into a large bucket attached to an aerial cable. The aerial cable moved the bucket across the river and over an open railroad car, where it was dumped. When the car was full, it was moved to the crushing plant at Micaville one-half mile away.

By 1929, over half the feldspar produced annually in the United States was produced in Mitchell, Avery and Yancey counties. The crude spar produced in 1929 in this area was over 100,000 tons and this was at a time of zero economic growth for the country. Most of the spar produced at that time was used in the glass-making industry. Most of the mining industry used a lot of manpower but offered few high-paying jobs. The spar industry changed that. Not only did they use many local tradesmen, but they also needed chemists, experienced machine operators and skilled workers. The volume was greater than most other industries so more machinery and larger processing facilities were required. The transportation industry grew rapidly as a result. The mining of feldspar had a real economic impact on the area.

The early mines required that before shipment, all spar had to be hand-picked and cleaned. This required a lot of manpower, and a lot of people were employed for this purpose. Mica was a saleable product and was kept. The bulk of the material removed from the mine was discarded as waste. With today's technology and needs, almost all the material is used. In yesterday's market, all dark minerals, with the exception of mica, were left in the dump. This included all dark-colored spars, garnet, smoky quartz, tourmaline, beryl, corundum, kyanite, etc. Old spar and mica dumps are a mecca for mineral collectors.

Spar suppliers were required to supply a clean, uniform product, and they did this by building laboratories and employing chemists. In 1930, a complete analysis of Western North Carolina spar going into the glass trade was as follows: silica - 69.00%; alumina - 18.00%; potash - 9.80%; soda - 02.70%; calcium - 00.35%; iron oxide - 00.10% and magnesium, a trace. It was desirable to keep the alumina count up and the silica count down. Iron content could not exceed one tenth of one percent. Occasionally an order would come in for spar to make amber glass. In that order, the iron content could be higher. As a rule, most Western North Carolina feldspar contains more potash than soda but there are exceptions.

At first, the spar was shipped to the customers as mined, after cleaning. After the railroad was built, crushing plants were built close by and then the spar was crushed and shipped according to customer specifications. It was placed in burlap bags and shipped bulk. The burlap bags were later replaced by paper.

In recent years, the abundant mineral silica, commonly known as quartz, has given Western North Carolina's feldspar mining a boost. Computers that a few years ago were large enough to fill a room, now are built small enough to sit on a desk top. Old inefficient generators are now replaced with small efficient alternators. Calculators, too heavy to carry, now are built to fit in one's shirt pocket.

To be able to produce electrical semi-conductors the manufactures must have pure silicon. The Spruce Pine pegmatites contain the purest quartz in the world. The computer and manufacturing industry, as well as electric forklift manufacturers have used the excellent quality Western North Carolina quartz. Perhaps electric vehicles of tomorrow will do the same.

Unimin Corporation in Mitchell County provides much of the world's needs of this high-quality silicate to be used in the production of fiber-optic cable and silicon for the production of rectifiers.

Corundum

The first systematic mining of corundum in Western North Carolina that I found information on was by a South Carolina native by the name of C.W. Jenkins, a Civil War veteran who mined Corundum Hill in Macon County. Also in 1890, Meminger and Hooker were mining the Muskrat Branch deposit on Shooting Creek.

Miners and investors were opening mines at several locations in the area. Colonel Harris was getting machinery together over at the Hog Rock clay deposit at Dillsboro. Heap and Clapp were getting their mica-mining operation together at the Sink Hole near Bakersville. Copper deposits were being explored everywhere. Gold deposits were being worked again.

Unfortunately, Mr. Jenkins chose the right mineral but at the wrong time. There wasn't a good market for abrasive corundum at the time and the economy was in a slump, so gemstones did not bring a good price. He did find a corundum crystal that weighed over three hundred pounds. After a couple of years, he ceased operation. In 1996, metallurgist Kempton Roll found records of how corundum was mined at Corundum Hill and how the process was used during the 1870s to manufacture the top for the Washington Monument.[1] The mine wasn't being worked at the time of the actual manufacture, but the corundum was mined during the period Jenkins owned the mine. Later, Hampdien Emerald and Corundum Company worked the mine for several years.

---

[1]Kempton Roll detailed this information in the Southern Appalachian Mineral Society newsletter, *The Mountain Mineral Monthly*, 1996.

When the country needed corundum, it was mined, separated and shipped to the processing facility. The other minerals, such as olivine, hornblend, limonite, serpentine and mica, were left as muck. At the Buck Creek Mine in Clay County, mineral collectors keep vegetation from growing.

Around 1909, International Abrasive Company purchased the mine and worked it for a short period. During World War I, Corundum Hill was the only mine in the United States supplying this critical mineral.

Industrial grade corundum is plentiful in Western North Carolina. At one time during the early 1900s, Western North Carolina mined all the corundum produced in the United States. Clay, Jackson, Transylvania and Madison counties were the main producers. Also, deposits were located in Swain, Mitchell, Yancey, Haywood, Buncombe, McDowell, Cleveland, Burke and Iredell counties. Mining of corundum continued until the early 1950s.

Common corundum was used as an abrasive. Using today's knowledge and machinery, it would be apparent that the surface had not been scratched. Corundum is formed deep under the earth's surface. The mining we have done until now has been removal of what has weathered to the surface.

The Corundum Hill Mine was located about seven miles from Franklin, off Route 64 East. The deposit was about 500 feet wide and about 1200 feet long. Just about anywhere you look in the area, some corundum can be found. However, Corundum Hill, as we know it today, seems to have held the heaviest concentration. Corundum Hill shouldn't be confused with Corundum Knob, located several miles to the west in Clay County.

Corundum was found in Macon County in 1867; many stories have been told about that deposit. Which one is the most accurate doesn't seem to be that important. The undeniable truth is that a lot of corundum was removed from the mine from the time C.W. Jenkins started the first serious mining in about 1871; it was last mined by Tex Donnel in the late 1970s. The corundum was first identified by professor C.D. Smith when Hiram Crisp showed him samples of exceptionally heavy red rocks that he had found while farming his land. When Crisp was told what the mineral was and that it was valuable as an abrasive, he was grateful—so grateful, in fact, he gave the professor half of the land where it was found. Cash wasn't something you just found laying around in those days, so people paid with what they had. In most cases, it was with farm products but in rare instances as this one, it was part of the farm itself. They both were happy but knew nothing about mining, so they sold the mineral rights to Ward and Jinks Mining Company for five thousand dollars. Ward and Jinks built a crushing plant near the closest water source, which was Cullasaja Creek, about a mile and a half down the hill from the mine. A flume line was built to carry the corundum from the mine to the mill. Water from the creek was used to clean the mineral and power the crusher. The mine was operated for about two years by Ward and Jinks using this setup and produced a little more than two hundred tons of powder. There must have been many cabinet and gem specimens discovered and kept, but apparently no records were maintained. During early corundum mining, crushing plants were built at Sapphire in Macon County and Buck Creek in Clay County.[2]

In 1878, a doctor by the name of Lucas along with his stepsons, Frank and George Bidwell, upgraded the grinding plant from gravity

[2]"Corundum and Peridolies in North Carolina," North Carolina Geological Survey, Volume 1, by state geologist Dr. Joseph H. Pratt, 1905.

water to steam power. After the modifications were completed, mining of the corundum was commenced again. Routine workdays were twelve hours long. Today's miners mine huge amounts of material and then separate what they mined, keeping what is marketable. Miners at that time could not afford that luxury. The vein was closely followed, mining only what was necessary. Only corundum was sent to the crusher. What dirt or foreign matter remained was washed off before being crushed.

At Corundum Hill, most of the mining was by open pit but some was underground. On the southern boundary of the deposit, a rich vein was found and mined for a distance of about thirteen hundred feet before it played out. It was called the Big Vein. The author imagines there was a nationwide search for a name before someone came up with that one. The Big Vein was worked by open pit and underground shaft. The total length of underground works was estimated to have been about one mile. On the northeast corner was the Zeb Jones Underground Works. The ore from the Zeb Jones contained about forty percent corundum.

During that period, the mine was producing up to three hundred tons of ground corundum per year and was selling for over two hundred dollars a ton. The mine closed again in 1900. The market was soft but some mining did take place between 1900 and 1914. In 1914, the demand rose rapidly. The Corundum Hill Mine was opened again and production gradually rose to its peak production year, 1917. It is said that the Big Vein alone produced two hundred and twenty-nine rail cars of ground corundum that year. If one was talking about bulk minerals, such as lime or olivine, that many carloads would not seem so large. However, this was ground-up rubies and sapphires. Gem-quality natural ruby can cost more than a diamond. Now it seems like that was a lot of powder.

After World War I, the demand for corundum dropped. The mine was worked a little now and again over the years, primarily by hobbyists. It was worked some for vermiculite during the Depression. On January 26, 1965, Corundum Hill Enterprises was incorporated. For a period during the 1970s, the Marguerite Mining Company had a small-gem recovery operation going. It did not last long but some nice gemstones were reported to have been recovered.

During the early days of industrial mining, ore was hauled to the surface of the Big Vein at Corundum Hill on a muck car. The remainder of the journey to the crushing plant was by flume line. Logs beside the track were used to support the ceilings of the mine.

The Corundum Hill mining operations were better documented than most. Talk to anyone with an interest in minerals from the area and more than likely they will have a story for you about the mine. One could write a book about this mine and its workers alone. Other corundum mines that meant a lot to our national defense were Buck Creek and Corundum Knob in Clay County.

The main shaft at Buck Creek was off Perrys Gap Road about one mile from Route 64. It was first mined by North Carolina Corundum Company, starting in 1902. Blocks of corundum weighing up to 125 pounds were mined. That mine was a horizontal shaft.

Corundum Knob, just a little to the west and part of the same massive deposit, was mined to a lesser extent. The mining there was mostly open-pit. At the time, the country was dependent on corundum as an abrasive for private and military use. The modern nation needed to manufacture modern machinery. Other minerals, such as garnet, could be used to grind and polish soft material. Only diamond was harder than corundum and most diamond had to be imported. During a war, that is a bad situation to be in. Western North Carolina came to the rescue. During World War II and the Korean War, Clay County supplied the need. The author heard that at one time Buck Creek was the only mine in the U.S. supplying the national need.

In 1902, the first large-scale mining of corundum on Buck Creek was by North Carolina Corundum. That company was owned by Detroit businessmen. Very few rubies were found while mining Buck Creek, but several were and still are being found on Corundum Knob. The processing factory is no longer there but that area today is a popular mineral collecting spot for people nationwide. Those deposits are called dunites.

Dunite deposits dot the landscape of Western North Carolina counties from Tusquitte Creek in Clay County, where deposits are exposed in road cuts. Small corundum crystals can be found in farmers' plowed fields. On the west bank of Lake Chatuge on Route 69, where rubies and sapphires have been found, the narrow band strikes east to Franklin and Avery County. Associated with those deposits are olivine, corundum (ruby and sapphire) talc, topaz, chromite, rutile (titanium oxide) serpentine and peridot (gem olivine), to name a few.

The olivine mine located at Daybrook, recently worked by Aimcor and now Unimin, was first mined for chromite by G.D. Ray during the 1880s, according to the *Asheville Democrat*'s Dec. 5, 1889 issue. During World War I, it was mined again for chromite. Over the years a market was developed for olivine. During World War II, a group of Chicago businessmen financed the Industrial Minerals Corporation of Burnsville. The group leased 300 acres of the Day Brook-Mine Hill property from the Ray heirs for the purpose of mining olivine and chromite. New machinery was installed during 1942 and mining commenced and continues today.

There are also many trace minerals found in dunite deposits, such as nickel. Around the turn of the century, a nickel ore processing plant was built at Webster. The nickel ore, deweylite, was located in the olivine formation. The operation was not profitable and was closed soon after opening.[3]

Most of the dunite deposits did not contain large amounts of corundum. The minerals in those deposits are primarily magnesium with no free silicate. Corundum is aluminum oxide and contains no silicate. If it was formed where there was a lot of free silicate (not silicon), a few atoms probably would smuggle themselves into the crystal structure. Aluminum silicate would be formed instead of aluminum oxide, a different mineral with a different crystal structure and with two different hardnesses. That mineral is known as kyanite.

Where the minerals come together is called the contact zone. Many different but related minerals were common. If there was free iron, the kyanite probably would have been staurolite.

Dunite minerals were formed deep within the earth's surface, where water under pressure can become so hot it melts quartz and other minerals. At that temperature, water is no longer called water but water substance. In a liquid state, these minerals separate themselves according to specific gravity. Normally the Earth's crust is weathered away or small cracks form, lowering the pressure gradually. As the temperature drops, crystals are slowly formed. If there is a rupture and the minerals are spewed towards the surface,

[3]Herman J. Bryson, *Mining Industry of North Carolina from 1929 to 1936*, Economic paper number 64, 1937.

the minerals will cool rapidly. Only small crystals will form, if any. There was and still is a lot of chemistry going on down there. Over the years, some of these dunites have exposed themselves. Those are the ones that have been mined for minerals that have been needed so badly. Those deposits are the ones that have provided all those beautiful gemstones. The author wonders how many corundum hills are just inches from the surface waiting to be discovered.

Kimberlite, the matrix of diamond, is a dunite. Diamonds have been found in the area. Think about it when you go on a picnic; look at those rocks. That could be a dunite you are standing on.[4]

---

[4]If interested in locating gemstone mines in North Carolina, an excellent list of references can be found in *Mineral Collecting Sites in North Carolina* by Wilson and McKenzie (North Carolina Geological Survey, Information Circular 24, Raleigh, N.C.), 1978, p. 20.

Copper Mining

Copper has been mined primarily in Ashe, Jackson, Haywood, Alleghany, Madison, Watauga and Swain counties. Native Americans mined copper in Western North Carolina for their own use. De Soto's army mined some and other Spaniards mined copper for over one hundred years. When the settlers came, they mined small quantities for their own use and to trade. By 1883, there were twenty-three operating mines in Western North Carolina. The mines prospered until the turn of the century.

The Ore Knob Copper Mine in Ashe County was closed during the Civil War and for a few years after. It was known that there was a rich copper deposit there. Copper was needed but investment money was scarce. During 1870, some investors from Baltimore, Maryland purchased the Ore Knob Mine and 500 acres of surrounding property. Ore Knob was remote, with few roads. Machinery had to be brought in. It took until 1873 before mining commenced.

During the next ten years, two new shafts were sunk and three hundred thousand tons of copper was mined. Over the years, the mine was opened and closed several times. The price for copper dictated the opening and closing. If the price of copper went up, then the mine opened; if it fell, the mine would close.

The Nipissing Minerals Company owned the mineral rights on the mine property from 1953 to 1962. The last company the author has knowledge of that mined there was Appalachian Sulphides. The ore of copper, chalcopyrite, was mostly depleted by 1962 so the mine was closed. When the mine closed, the support community of Ore

Knob was virtually abandoned. Today, the area surrounding the mine is primarily farmland with the majority of that being ornamental shrubbery.

Another early copper mine was the Pensacola Copper Mining Company, formed by a group of businessmen and miners during the 1850s. Some of these men were residents of Pensacola, North Carolina. Their names were: Robert P. Ray, John R. Crawford, James S. Rhea, Madison M. Bowman, Jacob Thomas, Thomas Crawford, William C. Ammons, George F.C. Ammons, Lawson Gifford, John Fleming, Joseph Spurgon, James Cragg, Landen C. Haynes, James W. Dedrick, Thomas Spurgon, Joseph Rhea, John Harley, Richard Deakins, William Lewis, John F. Preston and Matson Crawford.

Haynes and Dedrick are shown to each have one share. A receipt, dated November 3, 1855, found with other papers read, "received of J.W. Garland, $5.00 toward my work in the Pensacola Copper Mining Company in which Leander Ray is treasurer." These papers were part of the John Wesley Garland estate and were submitted to the *Yancey Common Times* by Lloyd Bailey and printed there on March 17, 1993.

Being a native of Pensacola myself, this came as a surprise to me. I knew there had been active copper mining in most Western North Carolina counties but very little is known about copper mining in Yancey County. It is known that Copper Hill, Tennessee experts were brought in to help evaluate local deposits.

I talked to Don Ray, a Pensacola native, about the Pensacola Copper Company. He told me that he had been to one of the old copper mines on the Rocky Fork of Cattail Creek. You could find small green specks of copper in the dump if you looked closely. One of Don's ancestors worked the mine for a period of time. His name was Will Ben Ray.

I have found no record of a local processing plant of copper. The ore would have been shipped by wagon. Western North Carolina roads of the 1850s must have made this task slow and expensive. The ore of copper, chalcopyrite, is found in hornblend schist, which is plentiful throughout Yancey County. The percentage of copper in the ore is very low. The pantia coating, also called copper bloom, can sometimes be seen in weathered rock. Unless the percentage of copper is high, the green-blue film will weather away after a few years. During the summer of 1994, I searched the area of Rocky Fork where Don told me the old mine was. I located the old dump, which was small. Without doing tests, I think the ore would not yield over five percent metallic copper. I have found no record of native copper deposits in Western North Carolina.

Yancey County neighbors to the west also had copper. In 1870, A.T. Freeman and Company was operating the Bear Creek Copper Mine in Madison County. Haywood and Jackson counties had the Waryhut, Cullowhee, Savannah, Shell Ridge, Scotts Creek, Sugarloff, Panther Knob, Wolf Creek, Blue Wing, Lincoln and Graham Copper Mines. Besides the Fontana and Hazel Creek, Swain County also had the Fonney. Neighboring counties to the east and north had copper deposits that were mined.

Alleghany had the Peach Bottom. Ashe had Elk Knob, Miller, Cooper Knob and Ore Knob. Further to the west, the Fontana Copper Company produced 15,000,000 pounds of metallic copper during 1929. That was the best year ever for the Fontana Copper Mine. The ore from this mine yielded eight percent. The ore was loaded onto rail cars at the mine and shipped to the Tennessee Copper Company for processing. The copper ore from Hazel Creek near the Fontana site yielded twelve percent but the Depression brought this operation to a halt before it ever got off the ground.

During the 1920s, the North Carolina Flux Company was operating approximately forty mines. One of these mines was at Cullowhee. Although it seems that a mining company of this size would have generated tons of information, I have found very little.

The ore from the Cullowhee Mine yielded seven percent. The Tennessee Copper Company leased this mine in 1929, just in time to shut it down for the Depression. After all, how were we going to have a decent Depression if everyone continued to work?

During the early 1920s about 10,000,000 pounds of copper were mined from Western North Carolina. Except for Fontana, all copper mining ceased in 1929. The Fontana Copper Mine now lies at the bottom of Fontana Lake.

The author is unaware of any copper being mined today in Western North Carolina.

Graphite, Chromite, Columbite & Lead

Graphite has been mined in Western North Carolina to be used for stove polish, foundry facings, pencils, dry cell batteries and lubricants. We have foliated graphite deposits scattered throughout Western North Carolina.

At the turn of the century, George Moon owned the National Graphite Company. He operated a mine at Busick in Yancey County. Another mine was operated at Graphite in McDowell County. Today, there isn't any graphite being mined in Western North Carolina but one of the area's leading manufacturing plants is Great Lakes Carbon Company, located in Burke County.

Chromite of excellent quality exists in Western North Carolina. Chromite is the only ore used to produce chromium. It was also used in fine paints. Surprisingly, very little commercial mining of this mineral existed in the region.

Columbite, used in the manufacture of fine surgical steel, was mined in Yancey County. I was told by John Bennett of Bald Creek that as a young man, around 1910, he drove a team of mules and hauled the ore from the mine on Jacks Creek to Burnsville. That mine was probably located on Upper Pigpen Creek in Yancey County.

Lead was a necessity to early settlers of Western North Carolina. Pioneers found deposits of lead for their own use, making bullets and cooking utensils. If they did not have their own mine, they would purchase it from those who did.

If an old-timer starts to talk about minerals, he or she will usually talk about lost gold, silver and lead mines. According to legend, there were lead mines near Table Rock, Linville Gorge and in the Unaka Mountains. Commercial deposits of lead were mined near Flat Top Mountain in Yancey County and Mackey Mountain in McDowell County. Today almost all of North Carolina's lead is imported, as are many other minerals. Western North Carolina has those minerals but cannot compete with the cheap labor and the lack of pollution and safety controls in other countries.

During the late 1800s, miners earned between seventy-five cents and one dollar per day. The largest competition on the world market was India. Their workers earned less than ten cents per day. Even at that low scale, North Carolina was better off financially but had trouble competing on the world market.

Barite

Barite is barium sulfate. Sometimes because of its appearance and weight, it is called heavy spar. Barium is a Greek word meaning "heavy." Over the years barite has been used for many things and still is in demand. Barite melts at low temperature and has the properties which make it an ideal flux for the manufacture of copper and welding filler rods. When barite is mixed with nickel, a strong alloy metal is formed. Barite was used in the manufacture of vacuum tubes.

Barium nitrate is used in the manufacture of fireworks. Barium sulfide is used in the manufacture of luminous paint. Barium chromite is used in paint and matches. Barium monoxide is used in making sugar. Barium peroxide is used to make hydrogen peroxide. Barium sulfate is used in intestinal-tract X-rays. The radiation will not pass through and the body will not absorb the barium. Powdered barite is used as a flame retardant, paper filler and in rubber and paint. Today, one of the major uses of barite is within the well-drilling industry. At extreme depths, the length of drilling rods would become so great they could break under their own weight. Pockets of high-pressure gas would be released to the surface. When mixed as a mud and the well filled, the heavy mineral helps float the rod and seal the well.

I have not confirmed this, but was told there were three cars of barite shipped from the Stackhouse Mine weekly. One car went to a grain-milling company. Supposedly, the barite was used as a filler and was heavier and cheaper than the wheat ground to make flour. I was greatly relieved to find out that they only bought the best barite, as it remained white throughout the baking process. If the barite had been contaminated with other minerals, their colors would have been present in the final product. Now I know why Mom's biscuits had a white powder on top that would not brown and powdery pockets throughout. Since our bodies do not absorb or digest barite, I suppose there was minimal risk. Barite is no longer added to flour. At the time, I suppose that practice, if true, was common knowledge. I found it interesting. The list of uses goes on, but I think by now you know there were and are many.

In the mid-1880s, a crushing plant was built at Warm Springs (Hot Springs). That was the start of a mining industry in the area that would last about 50 years. The area where the barite was located wasn't that large but several locations were mined. Some of them were at Stackhouse, just east of Sandy Bottom, Doe Branch, Spring Creek Mountain, northeast of Bluff. Several locations at Walnut Gap were mined.[1]

The largest and most productive area was Stackhouse in Madison County, North Carolina. The 20th century had just begun when Henry Moore began mining the Clondike Mine, located in that deposit. Over the years, many other shafts were sunk in that deposit. Shortly after mining of the Clondike commenced, a dam was built across the French Broad River to power a crushing plant. The grinding apparatus was a large drum where the mineral was ground by the bumping together action as the drum was rotated. That system proved to be ineffective and later would be tried with the same results by the spar industry. After several changes, the grinding plant became effective.

Henry Moore had named his company Carolina Barite. At 10 a.m., May 28, 1910, the officers of Carolina Barite met to adopt resolutions to incorporate. The officers were Henry G. Moore from Stackhouse, North Carolina, Albert G. Stillwell of New York and P.A. McElroy from Marshall, North Carolina. On June 10, 1910 the company offered the public 3,741 shares of stock. Mining by Carolina Barite continued at Stackhouse at a steady, profitable rate until the flood

---

[1]Location reference: North Carolina Division of Mineral Resources Bulletin 60, 1950.

of 1916. The mill was washed away and never rebuilt. I do not know where the barite was processed but mining of the Clondike as well as many other mines at that deposit continued at an accelerated pace until 1927. The Clondike was around 350 feet deep and had produced three hundred thousand tons when depleted.

That wasn't the first time I had heard of the 1916 flood. When I heard about it again it reminded me of a story told to me by Norman McCray, my wife's uncle. Norman was a young man when the McCray family was in the process of moving from Flag Pond, Tennessee to Sweet Water in Clay County, North Carolina. Their plans were to move their belongings to Marshall, North Carolina by mules and wagons. There they loaded everything onto the train for the trip to Murphy. The rivers began to rise before they got to Marshall. One of their mule teams and wagons was washed away. They did get on the train to Murphy before the height of the flood reached its maximum.

Since this story is about mines, miners and minerals and not floods, mules and wagons, I will get back to mining of barite in Madison County. Other deposits mined in Madison County were on the A.G. Butts property at Sandy Bottom, and the B.W. Gahagan Mine located north east of Walnut Gap. This mine was worked to a depth of about 200 feet and produced around thirty thousand tons.

Rollins Chemical Company mined several locations on Long Mountain at Bluff. That mine was also worked to a depth of about 200 feet. Mine Ridge was mined for barite to a lesser degree by various mining interests. To my knowledge, barite is not mined in North Carolina today, but Sazorite Mineral Company has a grinding and warehousing facility at Tomotla near Murphy.

The Clay Industry

The porcelain clay industry owes much to Colonel C. J. Harris of Dillsboro. Colonel Harris was mining kaolin from the Hog Rock Mine, four miles southeast of Dillsboro before the turn of the century. The Hog Rock Mine had an average of 60 percent recovery. Mines in Mitchell County had a recovery rate of about 20 percent. In later years, as new locations were found and recovery methods were better, the yield became much higher. The Hog Rock Mine played out after twenty-eight years of operation.

Colonel Harris knew of the vast deposits in Yancey, Mitchell and Avery counties, but mining them could not be considered. There was no transportation other than wagon. When the railroad was started towards Mitchell County, he got serious about the clay deposits in the Toe River Valley. In 1906, the Edgar brothers of Metuchen, New Jersey built a small clay operation at Penland. Colonel Harris bought them out in 1908. That same year he started the Sparks Plant at Minpro. By the mid-1930s, the deposit had been worked to a length of 1,200 feet and to an average width of 110 feet to 120 feet. Intermont China Clay of Penland sold out to Harris Clay in 1919.

The C.J. Harris plant at Ingalls has been worked continuously from 1937 until today. The plant has been sold many times over the years. Today, the Unimin Corporation owns the mine and processing plant. The clay plant was closed in 1993. Unimin continues to mine the deposit in 1997.

Carolina China Clay began operation in 1931. Organized by Harry Bailey and located at Penland on a site formerly worked by the Edgar brothers, the Bailey estate had at least seven deposits of clay to work. During the Depression years of the 1930s, the market for ceramic clay was not strong. The world economy kept the demand low. Also, we had not equipped the processing facilities to properly clean the product. During that era, annual sales rarely exceeded 22,000 tons.

No one knows for sure when the first clay was mined in Western North Carolina. If that was known, one would be very close to knowing when the first natives made their homes here. It is known that they mined clay in the area to be used for making containers, pipes, ornamentals and many other things as settlers moved in from the east.

When Thomas Griffith came into the area and kept a diary as he mined clay for Josiah Wedgwood in 1767, the mining of porcelain clays in Western North Carolina was quite extensive. Even though records of early clay mining are hard to find, we know clay was being mined long before Josiah Wedgwood. During that period, there were ceramic manufacturers scattered along the settlements of the east coast using the clay. Settlers had built homes on the east slopes of the Blue Ridge Mountains, including the Toe River Valley.

Even less talked about is mining that has taken place for pottery, brick and tile clay. This mining and manufacturing industry has been large and was active until recent years. Boreing Brick, formerly Moland Drysdale at Fletcher, was probably the last to close. A couple of the Madison County red-clay miners were Hot Springs Brick Company, Shale Clay Brick and Tile Company and Hot Springs Tile Company. Hot Springs Tile Company became a corporation March 22, 1907. Shale Clay Brick and Tile Company became a corporation August 30, 1913. Its mine and manufacturing facility was located two miles west of Hot Springs at the community of Attingers. The formal corporate papers said they could: mine shale clay to manufacture brick, terra cotta pipe and roofing; mine, prepare for market and generally deal in minerals, ores and clays; build and operate a water-powered electrical plant to supply power needed. The officers were John Jensen, D.H. Harris and James E. Rector. Hot Springs Brick was located at Shalesville. It was incorporated to mine clay and manufacture brick for building and paving, terra cotta pipe and generally deal in earthenware, porcelain, china, queensware, slate, tile, marble, lime, plastics, and building material. This company had been around awhile before they incorporated August 3, 1915 and the officers were B.G. Nicholson and H.P. Richler of Hot Springs and James E. Rector from Asheville.

Around the turn of the century there was a brick company located at Brickton in Henderson County named J.C. Shenell Brick Company. On August 4, 1914, its name was changed to Brickton Brick.

Pottery clay was mined at Arden, Candler, Hickory and Weaverville. Shale clay was mined in Madison and Henderson counties.

The mainstay of the porcelain clay has been kaolin. Halloysite has also been important, but to a lesser degree. Whenever people talk about minerals, they will normally refer to the group by the common group name. Some people will refer to minerals by their precise name. So many names can become confusing. However, most people would not refer to emerald as beryl. Emerald is beryl with just a little chromium—enough to change the color, but not enough to change the crystal structure.

Each mineral is given a name, physical properties and chemical composition. Whenever the chemical composition changes enough to change the color, a new name is given. That change is extremely important to many people, but to most it is not. For instance, kaolin clay came from albite feldspar. Halloysite clay came from the plagioclase base group of feldspar. The Cornwall England Ball Clay Mine came from the oligoclase series feldspar. Kaolin is also known as Carolina China Clay. The primary difference between kaolin and halloysite is the crystal structure. Halloysite clay has far fewer impurities.

Is all kaolin the same? According to some reports, there are six varieties or groups. These six are identical in composition but differ in crystalline structure. Kaolinite, the most popular, is believed to be a composition of all the varieties. During the 1940s and 1950s, primary kaolin sold for about $22.50 a ton. Primary kaolin, the type found in Western North Carolina, was created where it now rests. Secondary kaolin washed down from where it was formed and settled in lakes. Secondary kaolin sold for about $9 a ton. Impurities render secondary kaolin unsatisfactory for the manufacture of china, but there was a market for it in the ceramic industry. In 1952, 762,000 tons were sold from North Carolina's Piedmont.

Even though the large Hog Rock Mine was closed, Western North Carolina led the nation in clay production through World War I and the Roaring '20s. The clay deposits of Western North Carolina were mined heavily and production expanded daily. Spruce Pine pegmatite district led the way. Companies such as Carolina Products, Pollard Clay and Carolina China Clay were formed. Franklin Kaolin was formed December 24, 1904 in Macon County, North Carolina. Iotla and Gurney Clay were also located there.

In 1925, Yancey Clay was said to be the best in the world. Production for the county that year was 250,000 tons. Kaolin was leading production, with red-brick clay following a distant second for Western North Carolina.

The clay Josiah Wedgwood purchased from the Cherokee cost him several thousand dollars per ton delivered to England. In 1925, local primary kaolin sold for $5.00 per ton F. O. B. (user-paid freight). During the 1940s to 1950s, primary kaolin sold for about $22.50 per ton F. O. B. Secondary kaolin sold for $9.00 per ton.

The Harris Clay Mine and Processing Plant at Micaville was a typical kaolin operation of the time. The mine was located on the hill just east of Micaville. When possible, the processing plant would be located down grade and close to the mine, as was the plant at Micaville. When possible, water would be used to mine the clay and scrap mica. Water was not readily available in large quantity here but machinery was, so it was mined and loaded with large loaders into a flume line. Gravity-flow water washed the alaskite down the flume to the processing plant located at the Backus Rail Siding on the banks of the South Toe River. There it would be processed through a series of screens and settlings.

Small quantities were warehoused but most were loaded onto waiting rail cars. Through the 1920s, the industry did not have a reliable method to remove the micro-size mica from the clay. That was a serious problem for the industry.

The Micaville deposit, as with most deposits in the area that have been mined, provided millions of tons of alaskite. When the mine was depleted, the equipment from this mine was moved to the Lunday deposit.

The company store at Micaville still stands and is used today. That was a typical clay operation. All the essentials were there—the needed mineral, water, gravity, transportation and a market. The market was there, but the price was not good and did not change much until about 1936.

Early on, ceramic manufacturers could not depend on the quality of the clay. One load might contain 90 percent pure clay, which was not good but was acceptable. The next load might contain 60 percent clay and could not be used. Non-uniformity, the lack of plasticity and low dry strength rendered it almost useless. Worst of all, the clay was subject to turn to a pile of dust when fired. Most ceramic manufacturers believed the only way to use the clay was to mix it with English Ball clay. The profit was very low and money was not available for research. English clay continued to dominate the market. English Ball clay came from Cornwall, England, derived from orthoclase feldspar.

In 1927, a Canadian by the name of Harry Gaines came up with a method to separate and save the mica. Previously, the mica that was separated was not clean enough to save so it was disposed of by washing into streams. That discovery by Gaines was a major boost, but more had to be done if the clay was going to be competitive on the world market.

The clay still had problems and the Tennessee Valley Authority's top ceramic engineer, R.E. Gould, believed the problem was with contamination and not the clay itself. He set out to show that proper refining would change the physical state of the product. By the early 1930s, he had proven local clays were far superior to imported clay. The plasticity allowed pieces of ware to be molded in four minutes—these would take up to an hour using the best imported clay. After Harry Gaines developed the flotation separation method and R.E. Gould proved the clay had to be clean, there was no doubt North Carolina had the best clay in the world. The Kaolin Corporation built its facility at Ingalls using the latest technology. The king of clay, Harris Mining, was not about to take second place.

The old equipment that had been moved from Micaville to Lunday in 1921 was updated or replaced in about 1935. The clay now produced by those companies at those facilities was 99 percent pure. The world porcelain industry beat a path to our door, at least after the Depression. After Harris got their Lunday factory back into operation and it proved to be a good decision, they commenced modification of all their plants to include the other four they owned in Yancey. Harris Clay produced huge amounts. Geological reports showed all the deposits they mined contained over a million tons. All other clay operations upgraded their equipment or fell by the wayside.

Halloysite is another porcelain clay that was mined in the area. I mentioned it before but I think it deserves a little more information. Halloysite was first identified in Belgium in 1926. The first mining of that mineral in this area was about 1913. I do not know the exact location, but it was mined for aluminum sulfate content.

J.K. Patton of Celo in Yancey County was the first to successfully market it as a porcelain clay. He was working a mica mine located on J.R. Sluder's farm at Alexander in Buncombe County. The mine contained large amounts of this snow-white, silky mineral. How he went about finding a market is not clear, but he temporarily put mica mining on hold and commenced to mine clay.

The clay was mined by cutting it into blocks and shipping it directly to the user because cleaning, grinding and concentrating were not needed.

There must have been another deposit of minerals close to the halloysite. The mica J.K. Patton was mining would not have come from that deposit. Halloysite normally has a very low, if any, mica content. Eventually Harris Clay worked that deposit until exhausted. The mine was backfilled.

Spruce Pine Mica mined the Carter Ridge deposit in Mitchell County. There were many companies that mined halloysite, but the largest producer was probably Spruce Pine Mica.

The Bethel Clay Mine, located in Haywood County, was worked by Harris Clay up until about 1918. It is thought that deposit contained halloysite.

Harry Gaines was given credit for development of the flotation separation method, but it is only fair to say at least one clay operation in Penland was using their own flotation separation system before Gaines became known. I wanted to get more information on this operation but up until now I have accumulated very little.

In 1937, Carolina Kaolin Corporation printed a brochure[1] to send out to their prospective customers. Naturally, they tried to convince the kaolin users that Carolina Kaolin was the only company that could produce the quality and quantity desired. Even though their sparkling new modern factory, located in Avery County, was impressive, there were other older producers in the area, such as Carolina China and Harris Clay.

Why was Carolina kaolin so well known and desired? In remote American Colonial days, our English forefathers acknowledged the superior quality of the Southern primary kaolins. In 1768, William Cooksworthy, an English porcelain producer, first patented "hard paste porcelain." He did so after he had developed very fine porcelain made entirely from kaolin clay obtained from the Carolinas.

Josiah Wedgwood, referring to Carolina shipments, published statements expressing fear "that unless materials of similar quality were found in England, the manufacture of fine tableware would pass from England to the Colonies where excellent kaolin can be secured." The Bureau of Mines Publication No. 53 from 1913, "Mining and Treatment of Feldspar and Kaolin in the South Appalachian Region," quoted a well-known authority of that time, Arthur S. Watts, as follows: "The Bureau investigations show that there can be no doubt of the United States being able to supply all requirements (from the South Appalachian field) for domestic consumption and that the quality of kaolin

---

[1]*Carolina Kaolin, A Modern Industrial Romance*, Spruce Pine, N.C.,1937.

now available in this region is exceeded by none. The use of these products (Southern kaolin and feldspar) will make possible a grade of ware not approachable by the use of the finest foreign materials." Authorities went so far as to prophecy an eventual transfer of much of the pottery production to this raw production field.

Western North Carolina had the finest clay located close to railroad transportation and ample manpower, but until after the Depression, the United States was still partially dependent on foreign kaolin to supply the porcelain manufacturers.

During the turbulent '20s, a delegation of ceramic makers, co-operating with geologists and experienced miners, set out to verify the claims that the Southeastern Appalachian Mountains contained primary kaolin not excelled anywhere in the world.

The Carolina Kaolin brochure said this: Desultory mining in the mountains had continued for many years without locating a large source of supply. Crude operations were producing small tonnages of non-uniform, off-color micaceous clays, mainly from improperly mined dike formations. The ceramic manufacturers were inclined to disparage the product. I do not suppose a simple "Try Our Clay" would have been adequate.

Locating and mapping the Avery County field, located on what is today Brush Creek and next to the Avery County airport, cost the group a lot of money, but this was the Roaring '20s. Money was available and people were willing to invest.

Georgia and Florida had large sedimentary deposits of kaolin and they were being mined, but the ceramic producers were fully aware that in the drift through the ages from their mountain origin, these sedimentary kaolins had absorbed impurities and undergone physical changes, which precluded their general substitution for the imported residual kaolin so essential to many phases of the industry. The primary deposits in Carolina, of uniform quality and dependable quantity, looked the best. Several years of thorough, extensive and persistent investigation seemed to lead the investigation only to indefinite and unsatisfying conclusions in 1929.

Territorial examinations had extended from Alabama to Virginia. Private and state geologists had contributed to this effort.

The field of greatest promise had narrowed to the hills of North Carolina. With the collapse of the stock market, the plan of investigation was slowed. Some of their plans were temporarily put on hold or outright eliminated, such as a porcelain factory in the area. State Geologist H.J. Bryson gave encouragement and sound professional advice from the beginning and directed the search away from the rich, but small, spotty deposits of the upper Piedmont. His opinion that the mountains contained the larger and more dependable sources of primary deposits was later confirmed by other American and European geologists after many tests determined the actual size and quality of kaolin fields.

Porcelain manufacturers were constantly shipped carloads of free test kaolin. They would manufacture porcelain and a long line of porcelain collectors and connoisseurs of fine porcelain were waiting for the finished product. This lent prestige and encouragement to the undertaking. Carolina Kaolin spent large sums of money just to locate the most ideal deposit of kaolin in the world.

Even though I have been calling this group of people Carolina Kaolin, up to this point they had no name. They were a group of businessmen with a background in porcelain or mining with a common goal. Apparently the Depression caused some of the principals to lose their funds. In those days, a firm handshake and a person's promise was as good as gold, so the project went forward. The site was chosen. Over 4,000 acres were made available to be mined. What remained of the original effort became Carolina Kaolin.

Old land records tell much about the chain of events and people's thoughts at the time. On August 8, 1837, my great-great-great-grandfather, Bedford Wiseman, purchased much of the land where the clay field was located. He did not have the property surveyed nor did he have the deed recorded. This was common practice. Later my great-great-grandfather James H. Wiseman purchased much of the property from his father. On the 23rd day of May 1890, he had the property surveyed and deed corrected but still not recorded.

I have wondered why the flurry of activity occurred in 1890. I suspect Colonel Harris was in the area looking for high-quality clay.

I have no record of active mining of the deposit during the 1800s but some of the old deeds would mention that the mines located on the property would be sold with the property. The mineral rights must have changed hands in 1929. The deed was properly recorded on the 6th of December 1928. During that time they went from a handshake to a legal contract.

My idea is that the original planners already knew where this field was located. The Depression slowed the progress down, so while plans were being checked and implemented, this field and others were being tested and mapped. After all, Colonel Harris knew of and had tested this field at least thirty years earlier. It would not hurt to build up a little excitement while the Depression was wearing down.

American mining and processing methods at that time did not produce the ideal porcelain clay. The best methods were tried and improved, but it was still difficult to get the ceramics on the world market. Carload lots were shipped to Europe to be tested over a two-year period. As a result, the best-known American methods were combined with the process universally recognized as the world standard, that of the Zettlitz Kaolin Company in Karlsbad, Czechoslovakia. For more than fifty years, Zettlitz-processed kaolin had been recognized as the world's purest and most uniform kaolin and the legally recognized standard against which all others were measured. Zettlitz Kaolin conducted the most and toughest tests and placed the world's highest standards on their kaolin. Mr. R.E. Gould, general manager of Ciesche Fabrlyka Porcelany in Katowice, Poland, offered the services of the plant laboratory. This service was extremely valuable and appreciated. The American Ceramic Society, with the help of the Tennessee Valley Authority, conducted a study of all Tennessee Valley clays and provided this report to Carolina Kaolin, which was extremely helpful. In England, Germany and Czechoslovakia, some of the best-known laboratories were of assistance. In America, most research directors and laboratories of nationally regarded corporations associated with the industry provided assistance. The terrain in which the fields were located was described as a 4,500-acre tract located in a great kaolinized basin rimmed by the crest of the Blue Ridge and abounded in deposits of high grade potash feldspar, as well as quartz and mica.

The plant construction started around 1935. It was going to be a modern building, using only concrete, steel and glass. Approximately 300 construction workers were needed. About ninety-five percent were mountain people. This must have been extremely important to the area economy. The plant operation was to be directed jointly by American and Bohemian engineers. The plant site was to be where the community school had been for many years. Today, it is known as the School House Mine.

*   *   *

The geologic formations of the kaolin beds consist of two major types: metamorphic and igneous. The metamorphic rock of this bed was composed of gneiss and schist of Pre-Cambrian age, probably algonkian. The formations lie in a northeast-southwest direction and dip to the northeast and southwest.

The igneous rocks consist of two basic types, granite and pegmatite.

The granite was probably formed during the carboniferous period and was intruded into the Pre-Cambrian formation. The pegmatites occur in lenticular masses, cutting the granite and the Pre-Cambrian greisens and schists. They found that the pegmatites were composed essentially of feldspar, quartz and mica, with feldspar predominating. The uniformity of the large granite or alaskite intrusion accounts for the uniformity of the kaolin deposits. This was not a dike formation and in that respect it differed from the usual kaolin deposits found in Western North Carolina and other Southern Appalachian deposits.

Contamination of the kaolin was of major concern. If allowed to occur, the product could not be used. By this time, power machinery was available and it was put to use. Carolina Kaolin used a large power shovel to load the overburden on trucks and remove it from the field; also a contamination safety zone was created so surface water would not contaminate the main deposit. Drainage ditches were dug to collect and divert water.

The kaolin at first was mined at Brush Creek by selective hand labor to insure purity. The kaolin was loaded directly on conveyor belts and conveyed to the headhouse. From there it went to the crusher, then called a disintegrator. From there the finely crushed product went to the flotation separators called blungers. There the heavy minerals were removed. All minerals not completely crushed were removed. The kaolin slurry was then passed over a set of highly efficient screens by which the coarse mica was removed. The slurry continued on through a number of decontamination stages before reaching the concentrating tanks, where all free water was drained off. Then the kaolin passed through a press and came out as cakes. The cakes were passed through tunnel dryers and stored, ready for shipment. Every stage was monitored constantly. No kaolin would be allowed to pass that was not perfect. The clay was shipped to the customer by rail for many years. Carolina Kaolin guaranteed their product.

Carolina Kaolin later changed its name to Kaolin Incorporated. When the war came, Kaolin Incorporated sold out to Harris Clay. Later, Harris Clay was sold to the Unimin Corporation. Unimin offered ground mica and clay. The clay operation closed in 1993; at this time we can only speculate at the cause. The old Carolina Kaolin Plant was torn down and a new quartz processing plant built on the site. One thing that is known is that there is still plenty of the world's best kaolin in Western North Carolina. There is still a good market for high-grade kaolin, but it has been discovered that the real wealth is not in the clay itself but in the minerals found in the clay and spar. Those valuable minerals can be separated and sold for use in modern-day electronics.

Kyanite & Unakite

When Bleiniger and Riddle developed the first perfect spark plug of porcelain during World War I, through the inclusion of an alumina monosilicate in the body mix, the search was on all over the world for high-grade deposits of minerals of this type to fill the demand.[1]

Andalusite was discovered in California; dumortierite in Nevada and Washington State. Kyanite, the mineral best suited, was found in abundance in the mountains of Western North Carolina. Kyanite was spelled cyanite by many during that period. Minor deposits of kyanite were found in other states, also. Found in almost all Western North Carolina, the best deposits were near Burnsville, Black Mountain and Bakersville.

It is known that there were large deposits in most areas along the Blue Ridge Mountains, with probably the best gem quality in the world being in Buncombe County, just north of Milepost 361 on the Blue Ridge Parkway in the Craggy Mountain range. That deposit is mostly depleted.

Western North Carolina had the mineral that was needed to make the best spark-plug porcelain, but contamination was a major problem. In order to be used, the kyanite had to be almost pure when ground. Quartz and mica could be removed using the flotation process, but tourmaline and garnet formed in the crystal. Their specific gravity is almost identical to kyanite. These minerals contain iron and would be objectionable because of color and dielectric strength.

J.A. Pollard and his son, Lewis, built a kyanite grinding plant at Windom in Yancey County. It was named Pollard Clay and Kyanite. Pollard Clay was well known, but I have found very little information to show that Pollard Clay and Kyanite produced any kyanite. However, one old-timer who was around in those days told the author that Pollard Clay did mine kyanite, and the processing plant was at the same site as the clay plant. The larger kyanite mines were on Bill Allen Branch, White Oak Creek in Yancey County and Mills Creek in McDowell County. Woodys Ridge mine was located on the dividing ridge between White Oak and Upper Browns Creek. There is a lot of kyanite float in that area and at one time kyanite was mined near there. The old service roads have been closed in the area, so if you plan to visit, prepare for a long walk. Some of the marginal-producing mica mines in the same general area between Woodys Knob and Little Celo Mountain. At Bowditch were the Joe Goodin, Silvers, Bowditch and Ailers Creek.

In 1926, F.B. Ward mined for kyanite and sunk a shaft in a rich deposit near Bandana. At this time, little else is known about the operation.

Pearcy Threadgill, a native of Florida and resident of Pensacola in Yancey County, teamed with fellow Florida residents to form the Celo Mines Corporation. In 1934, they opened the Bill Allen Branch Kyanite Mine. The mine had been worked before but not to the extent it would be during the next ten years—the Depression had closed the earlier mining. During the 1930s, the price of the best grade of ground kyanite dropped to $36 a ton.

One kyanite mine and processing plant managed to continue operation during most of the 1930s. This mine and processing plant was located on the east side of Bolens Pyramid in Yancey County. The owners and operators were Celo Mines. Their best customer was the Laclede Christy Clay Products Company of St. Louis. Laclede Christy produced a cellular brick from the kyanite that was primarily used in furnace roofs. The mine closed for a while, but did produce again during the war.

In January 1942, the Defense Plant Corporation bought the kyanite mines from the Celo Mining Company. Mr. James McClure of Asheville was the Defense Plant president. Production was brought up to 300 tons of ore per day. Garnet was sold as a by-product.

During World War II, Mas-Celo Mines and Yancey Kyanite leased the mine from the Defense Plant Corporation. James McClure was president of Yancey Kyanite; V.L. Matson was in charge of the Burnsville office and Charles Rice was mine super-intendent over a crew of about 75 men. The equipment from Northstate Feldspar was set up at the mine. Its grinding plant at Micaville was for sale, and though the equipment was old and obsolete, Mas-Celo needed equipment in a hurry—the equip-ment could be moved and modernized faster and cheaper than building a new facility. Hence, the old North State Spar Crushing Plant was brought back to life as a kyanite crusher and separator.

By that time, many new uses had been found for kyanite, including low-alkali, heat-resistant glass to be used for the chemi-cal industry. Much kyanite was also needed for the war effort. At first, production was set at 300 tons a day; as the demand became greater, production increased to 500 tons a day.

Yancey Kyanite Company was active from 1934 to 1944. The mine yielded needle (sillimanite) and blade kyanite up to four inches long. The host (matrix) rock was primarily a dark gray mica gneiss (pronounced "nice"). The gneiss also contained biotite, muscovite, quartz, garnet, albitic feldspar, apatite, beryl, pyrite, pyrrhotite, chalcopyrite, galena, sphalerite, bornite and chalocite. Most of the minerals listed were not rich enough to concentrate and sell. Some that were mined and sold as byproducts include abrasive garnet and thermally luminescent quartz. Biotite domi-nated the mica, making it unsaleable—and there was no worthwhile market for scrap biotite. During that period, Earnes Briggs purchased all of Yancey Kyanite's mineral rights.

In 1943, N.E. Chute of the United States Geological Service conducted a detailed survey of the deposit. The report was never released to the public. The demand for industrial-grade kyanite dropped, and the mine closed in 1944.

The primary use of kyanite was furnace bricks. The demand for a mineral that would meet the standard required to build spark-plug insulators led scientists to the mountains and subsequently to the mining of kyanite. Kyanite can stand tremendous amounts of heat or chemicals without expanding, melting, warping or cracking. Kyanite was mined a lot, but compared to other minerals, it remained small.

The mica, feldspar and clay industry overshadowed the kyanite industry. Not a lot has been recorded about it. Gem-quality kyanite is collected today and commands a high price.

There are large deposits of unakite, a unique variety of granitoid, in Watauga, Avery, Mitchell, Yancey and Madison counties, where the Unaka Mountains are located. The majority of mined unakite has been used locally as road gravel. This mineral is also used in the jewelry industry, but there is no indication it has ever been mined for this purpose.

Other Minerals

Olivine has been mined over the years in Clay, Jackson, Yancey and Avery counties. In the past, olivine has been used for sand molds to pour castings and for fire bricks. Today, new uses have been discovered. It shows great promise in the agriculture industry. Recently, the author tried some on yard plants and not only did it make them greener, the bugs would not stay on the plant. Western North Carolina has a good supply of olivine.

Aimcor had several olivine mines in Western North Carolina and a processing plant at Daybrook in Yancey County. Aimcor sold their operations to Unimin Corporation in 1995.

Uranium became a widely sought-after mineral during the first half of the twentieth century; nuclear-powered electrical plants, X-ray machines, ships and national defense were the primary users. Apparently, no extensive mining of this product has taken place in Western North Carolina but small quantities have been mined, primarily in the northwestern counties.

Manganese is a valuable mineral that is not popularly known. Western North Carolina has this metal mineral, and it has been mined in the area for many years. The author knows of none being mined in the area today. Early uses were as a metallic dye used to give glass and pottery shades of violet, purple, green, brown and black. Also, it was used in bleaches and disinfectants. In recent years, as the demand for stronger steel has increased, the demand for manganese has also increased. When properly mixed with manganese, steel has ten times the strength of cast iron. Most manganese mined today is used in the production of iron and steel alloys. The deposit that perhaps was worked the most is located at Woodlawn in McDowell County. In the early part of the century, it was worked by American Mineral and Chemical Company from Raleigh, Clough Manganese from the District of Columbia and Weber Manganese from Philadelphia, Pennsylvania. Today, Woodlawn is being mined for lime and road gravel. Shut In Creek in Madison County also has a deposit of this valuable mineral that was mined for a short period of time. Dry Branch also had a deposit worked on in the same area of Madison County.[1] Apparently, the early mining there was around 1890.

Sand has been mined and used in large quantities since concrete construction came of age. Until large earth-moving machinery became available, most sand was removed from stream beds. Sand gives cement strength. The tough rock we have in Western North Carolina is ideal for this purpose. Unless someone decides it is a health or environmental hazard, the market will continue to be strong.

Tungsten, the hardest metal known, has been mined in North Carolina since the turn of the century and continued to be until recently. Little, if any, is being mined today. Tungsten has many uses, especially in our national defense. Drops in prices have caused mining operations to slow; the mineral is available when the market resumes. During the Depression years when Western North Carolina mine owners were paying little to nothing for labor and would not hire you even for that, the tungsten mines at Henderson were hiring and paying fair wages. Many experienced miners went to work there. The early tungsten mines were shaft mines but the later mines were open-pit.

Zircon has also been mined in the mountains. Most people think tungsten has always been used as the filament in electric light bulbs. It wasn't. The first filament (the part that glows) was made with zircon from Henderson County. Records show 3,208 pounds were mined and sold from that location in 1911. The mine was actually located at Zirconia. Mineral collectors have enjoyed rock hounding

---

[1]North Carolina Department of Conservation and Development Bulletin Number 60, 1950.

there for many years. Today, special permission is required before entering the private property.

Building-stone suppliers have sprung up all over Western North Carolina in recent years. In the past, if you wanted to construct something using rock, you went down to the river or out in the field and collected your own. Today, professionals mine many varieties. After the rock is mined, it is taken to a sorting and shipping yard, where it is shaped and sorted, then placed on wire-caged pallets. Today if you want construction rock, figure what quantity, size, color and strength you need. Drive down to your local rock supplier and pick out what you want. They will deliver.

An interesting fact is that much more building stone is shipped to the Northeast, where there are large deposits of granite and quartz, than anywhere else in the United States. The forefathers evidently passed on some of their mining ability.

Western North Carolina granite was mined to be used as gristmill grinding stones and had the reputation of being the best in the Southeast. It also has been mined and used for headstones and for gravel.

One would not think of gravel as being mined, but once you give it some thought, you realize it is probably the most mined product in Western North Carolina today. Gravel is mixed in cement for house and building foundations, for concrete and asphalt roads, and is used for gravel roads, railroad track beds and slingshot ammunition. Large gravel is sold as rip rap and used for erosion control. Due to the low cost, everyday use and abundance, not much thought is given to the gravel industry, but it is huge.

Another useful mineral mined in Western North Carolina is talc, which is used to make fire extinguishers, foot and body powders, cosmetics, ornamental carvings, molding release agents and marking sticks. Talc, or soapstone, was mined by Native Americans and used primarily for containers, pipes and jewelry. It is believed they also left messages scratched in talc outcroppings along their trails. This is highly evident at the track rocks near Blairsville, Georgia and many locations in Western North Carolina.

Early settlers used soapstone for cooking, water containers and headstones. When constructing a fireplace and chimney, normally soapstone was used for fire brick. The heat would cause native rock to crack and crumble. A lot of clay chinking was required to fill in the joints of native stone. Soapstone could be sawed to the dimensions needed. Due to the high density, it would hold heat long after the fire had died. When heated, it would not expand and crack. At first, having a soapstone fireplace was a status symbol; later it was taken for granted.

Before the Civilian Conservation Corp (CCC) built the present Carolina Hemlock Campground in Yancey County, there was a campground on the opposite side of the South Toe at the mouth of Colberts Creek. Most of the fire pits still stand. They were built with local soapstone.

The Hitchcock Corporation of Murphy, Cherokee County, was a major supplier of talc for many years. The author visited the vertical shaft mine once in 1965. The manager showed me several containers of powdered talc, each a different color and for a different customer in the cosmetic industry. When shipping, the color and grind had to match perfectly. The previously known Hitchcock Company sold out and became known as the Warner Corporation. In the 1970s, there were so many federal and state safety and environmental laws passed that the mine had to close. It had been mined intermittently since 1859.

For awhile, they tried mining talc at Hewitt near Nantahala to be used as marking stones for the steel fabrication industry. Foreign competition could put the product on the customer's shelf for about what it cost Warner to mine. Warner tried competing by extruding the ground mineral into sticks. That cut costs, but the market was lost to China. They no longer offer that product. In 1993, they were mining a brown mica shist at Hewitt, grinding and separating the product at their Murphy plant. They sell the finished mica product to the roofing industry for about $50 a ton.

Marble has played an important economic role in Western North Carolina for many years. White marble was mined at Marble in Cherokee County, located between Andrews and Murphy.

Columbia Marble had a large quarry and finishing plant at Marble. When mining, they would drill small holes close together in a straight

The factory and workers are gone; the marble is still here waiting.

line and use a small charge to blast. The blocks weighed several tons. A large crane mounted on tracks would lift the cube of marble and haul it to the saws, a row of diamond-tipped saws that looked like cross-cuts. Water was used as a lubricant and coolant. Once cut to slabs, they were moved inside and further cut by diamond-tipped circle saws. Next they were ground and polished to a mirror finish. They produced whatever the customer wanted—table tops, headstones, ashtrays and other products. The scrap was ground and sold as gravel. Columbia Marble closed the plant in the early 1980s.

Nantahala Talc Company of Murphy mines a beautiful pink marble at Hewitt, but it is ground and sold as gravel. A unique deposit of marble is located at Bandana in Mitchell County. During the late 1970s, Bud Phillips from Spruce Pine, Mitchell County, mined it for about ten years before the mine was closed because of environmental problems.

Western North Carolina has large quantities of beautiful pink, white and blue marble second to none, even Italy. When the world market increases its demand for marble, Western North Carolina will be able to fill the need.

Garnet has been also mined in Western North Carolina. Little Pine Garnet Mine in Madison County produced garnets for the abrasive industry for many years. Fine gem-quality garnets have been mined in Macon and Burke counties.

Asbestos had long been sought after by industry. Mitchell and Yancey counties provided a large portion of the supply needed. It is a long-fibered, strong and flexible mineral, an excellent insulator which can withstand intense heat. It was used as steam pipe insulation, in brake shoes, in plasters, protective clothing and many other uses.

Asbestos fibers can be carded, spun and woven much the same as flax, wool or silk. Perpetual lamp wicks made of asbestos were used by the Vestal Virgins of ancient Rome.

In the thirteenth century, Marco Polo found asbestos cloth in Siberia. However, asbestos did not become commercially important until about 1860. A little over a hundred years later we found asbestos has a bad side; it can cause cancer. Mining of asbestos had already ceased in Western North Carolina. Several tons were mined and abandoned beside the road going to the Goog Rock Spar Mine in Yancey County. That asbestos deposit was worked by several companies, including W.T. Hippey, Industrial Minerals and Powhatan Minerals of Asheville.

Mining and Milling Company of America, a New York-based company, did extensive testing of asbestos deposits located in the Yancey and Mitchell County area. Tests showed the deposits to be large enough to mine and the quality was high. The mineral was needed immediately. Mining was commenced in 1952, even before they had adequate facilities. Space was rented from United Feldspar. Walter Ruckeyser was in charge of the asbestos operation.

Scrap Mica Mining

The scrap mica industry in Western North Carolina has played a much larger economic role than the name implies. Before the turn of the century, large amounts of scrap were produced by the sheet mica industry and the material was treated as a nuisance. History about the development of this industry in Western North Carolina is scarce. When information is found, it is usually in the form of statistical figures.

Due to the large amount of scrap produced, a market was sought from the beginning just to use the existing scrap from the sheet mica and clay industry. At this time, feldspar and quartz were waste products. Also, mining the alaskite deposits located within the Spruce Pine, Shelby, Sylva and Franklin pegmatite districts for scrap mica had not been considered. Later, they were mined and processing plants were located there.

It appears that the first grinding plant of this area was erected on Beaver Creek near Spruce Pine about 1870. Since no mining of alaskite or mica schist for scrap mica was going on at the time, no concentration plants were needed.

Shortly after the Beaver Creek plant commenced production, David T. Vance built one at Plumtree. About the same time, another was built at Penland. Shortly before the turn of the century, Virginia got in on the act and built a crushing plant at Richmond. Crushing plants reduced scrap mica to the finished product, ground or powder mica.

In 1907, Macon County got its first crushing plant. Franklin Kaolin and Mica Company was mining the Iotla Mine for clay and sheet mica. They built a crushing plant to process the waste mica. Southern Mica eventually took control of the mine. When the on-hand sheet scrap depleted, they built Macon's first concentration plant.

English Mica of Spruce Pine built its first crusher plant in 1908. These early crushing plants used up the on-hand supply of scrap mica extremely fast. The market for ground mica was growing by leaps and bounds.

Alaskite was the name given to the minerals contained in many of the pegmatites. I did not find the specifications for alaskite but supposedly our deposits even though not exactly were close enough to be called that. Alaskite is spar that has been exposed to water and chemicals long enough to become soft (clay.) Quartz and mica would not decompose as quickly as spar; they were expected to be there, but to early clay miners, it was critical that the percentage not be high. Later, as separation methods were improved, that became less of a problem. Mica and silica became marketable later. Mining scrap mica would not take place for several years; the scrap from previous sheet mica mining had to be used. The miners knew of the huge deposits of small mica found in the alaskite and mica schists. The mica content of these often exceeded twenty percent.

An economical method to separate the mica had to be found and plants erected. This problem was figured out and the first concentration plant was built in Spruce Pine in 1910 by Charley Gunter. He sold the finished product to the English Mica Company. In 1950, there were sixteen concentration plants and six wet and five dry grinding plants in the area.

The concentration plants separated and cleaned the mica by crushing the hard minerals to powder, leaving the mica intact. The separating and cleaning were accomplished by screening and washing. This method was not efficient. Little or no mica smaller than one twenty-five thousandths of an inch was recovered. This size would simply fall through the screen and be removed as waste. A total of between fifty percent and eighty percent of the mica mined was discarded as waste.

Feldspar-flotation plants used the most efficient method. Flotation could recover practically all the mica and feldspar. Processing plants could afford to use this method since mica was a by-product to them. Flotation separation would not be available for several years to come yet.

The flotation method was much too expensive for general use. The North Carolina State Mineral Research Laboratory in Asheville came to the rescue. They developed the Humphrey Spirals. Up to eighty percent of mica was recovered using this method. The Humphrey Spirals was a simple, cost-effective apparatus, constructed in the form of a long, spiral trough. The length and slope could be adjusted to fit the material to be separated. The minerals, after being crushed, would be dumped into the trough at a steady, measured rate. As the minerals tumbled down the trough or spirals, the heavy minerals would displace the lighter ones and move to the outside. Slots at the bottom would direct the minerals to separate containers. To further separate the minerals, they could be recycled. Other methods have been perfected but the cost of operation prohibits use except where the mineral after separation has to be pure. Some of these are leaching, flotation separation, froth flotation and the Lewis flotation. The Lewis flotation is a recent invention, best used in the gold- mining industry, but it can be adjusted to separate most minerals.

After the mica was separated and cleaned, the product was still not ready for market. The next step was to wet grind, dry grind or microsize. Wet-ground mica brought the best price. Microsizing required a special grinding process and is discussed in a later section.

Wet grinding was accomplished in a chaser plant for many years with few changes. A chaser plant consisted of steel or wooden pans approximately ten feet in diameter and forty inches deep. The bottom of the pan was lined with end-grain blocks of wood. The preferred variety was oak, maple or black gum. Horizontal arms were attached to a central vertical shaft and large solid wooden rollers were placed on the arms. Normally, these rollers were thirty to forty inches in diameter and approximately twenty-four inches wide. The rollers could be raised and lowered, depending on the size of the batch or charge. Pressure was applied and the rollers turned at between twenty and forty revolutions per minute. Extreme heat would build up fast. Care had to be taken or the mica could be scorched and ruined. Plows followed the rollers to stir the charge and make sure no mica escaped the rollers.

Grinding started with a dry charge, adding water gradually until a stiff paste was formed. During this process, samples were taken to determine size, uniformity and quality. This process required from four to eight hours per ton, depending on the equipment.

From there it was dumped into wooden boxes called launders, where grit and large mica settled. Water was dumped into the vats. The overflow carried the fine mica to another vat. After settling, the water was drained off. The large mica from the first vat was returned to be ground again. Some plants at this time would filter the mica to remove large mica that had found its way through. It could also be run through a press to remove moisture.

Most plants skipped the last two processes and from the last vat sent the mica directly to the steam table. There it was dried. The dried mica was then run over a vibrating scalper screen, usually of about sixty to eighty mesh, to remove heavy particles that would damage the fine silk cloth of the bolting machine.

The bolting machines were similar to those used to bolt flour. After the mica was bolted to size specifications, it was packaged and ready for shipment. Even though this system was slow, it was used for many years with few changes.

Again, North Carolina State Minerals Research Laboratory, along with the Tennessee Valley Authority and private industry, developed a grinding method that was much faster. Dry-ground mica did not bring as much money per ton as wet- ground but the production cost was lower and lower-grade scrap could be used.

The process of cleaning and concentrating was basically the same for both wet- and dry-ground mica. When the mica left the cleaning and concentrating plant to be dry ground, it was taken to a hammer or attrition mill where it was reduced in size to meet specifications. Vibrating deck screens were used for sizing.

Large volumes of dry-ground mica could be produced quickly and cheaply. Not only did ground mica have to meet size and color specifications, it had to meet weight requirements. Wet-ground could not weigh over eleven pounds per cubic foot; dry-ground could not weigh over eighteen pounds. I suppose the weight requirement was to assure uniformity and purity.

Micro mica required a special grinding process. As the name suggests, the mica was reduced to an extra-fine powder from five to twenty microns. A lot of oil filters on today's modern engines would not pick this up if somehow it got into the car's crankcase. I do not know how many manufacturers in Western North Carolina produced micro mica.

The July 1947 issue of *Rock Products* described the process. It consisted of injecting high-pressure, super-heated steam into a shallow, circular grinding chamber where one-twenty-five thousandth of an inch or smaller mica was added at a steady flow. The steam entered through jets set at an angle to whirl around and cut across the rotating mica. As the particles become smaller, the centrifugal force no longer kept them to the outside and they gravitated toward the center, where the powder was collected.

Why would anyone would want to grind mica so small it was almost invisible to the normal eye? When mica is used in paint, it must be ground that small. The wet-ground and micronized particles, despite their smallness, still retain the characteristic platy structure of mica. When incorporated into paint, they overlap one another like shingles on a roof. As a result, mica-bearing paint produces good protection against corrosion and is often specified for metal surfaces exposed to air containing salt or chemicals. Almost all paint would be improved if mica were added but that would make paint too costly for ordinary application.

Prices for raw scrap and ground mica from North Carolina are quoted in the November 1952 *Engineering and Mining Metals Report* as: scrap, $32.00 to $35.00 per ton; wet-ground, $140.00 to $155.00 per ton; dry-ground, $32.50 to $70.00, all depending on quality.

In 1901, Western North Carolina sold 1,775,000 short tons of scrap mica at $8.00 per ton. This was the scrap from active sheet mica mines. To produce this amount of scrap the total production must have been enormous. In 1950, 48,193 short tons were sold at $26.58 per ton. The price of scrap mica reflected the economic conditions at the time. In 1920, scrap mica brought $32.47 a short ton. During the 1930s, it dropped to $11.47.

Over three hundred and twenty-five pegmatites have been worked for sheet and scrap mica with significant output in the Sylva-Franklin area alone. This does not include clay, feldspar and small insignificant mica operations, of which there were many.

Deneen Mica Company, founded by Fred Deneen, has supplied industry with a high-quality dry-ground mica since 1946. Deneen's processing plant is located on the east bank of the South Toe River at the corner of NC 80 and US 19 E. In 1992, Deneen stopped production. In 1994, Aspect Minerals purchased the Deneen Plant. As of 1997, Aspect is wet grinding mica there.

The Huber Corporation had a wet-grinding plant located on Bear Creek Road in Mitchell County. This plant has also been closed for a couple of years but in 1993 a crew reworked the plant in preparation of starting production again. Aspect Minerals is the new owner. As of 1997, that facility is also wet grinding mica.

The *North Carolina Department of Conservation and Development Bulletin* in 1953 listed a few of the scrap-mica deposits of Western North Carolina:

• The Iotla Bridge Mine, also known as the Bradley, is located in Macon County, 300 feet northwest of the Iotla Bridge at the point where NC 28 crosses the Iotla River. This was a scrap mica mine, first opened in 1905 and worked until 1947. There was a demand for this mica in 1947 and the Iotla was not depleted, but removal of the mica was cost-prohibitive due to the extreme depth of the mine.

• Grassy Ridge, also known as the Big Flint, is located in Jackson County, two miles southeast of the community of Balsam. This mine was first mined for scrap by A.W. Davis in 1932. A.W. Davis must have loved mining. When he was laid to rest at Sylva, the family placed a large beryl crystal and several other pegmatite minerals in his headstone. I have not found records to indicate when this mine was last worked, but Franklin Mineral Products held the lease as late as 1953. This mine also contained high-quality feldspar.

• The Mill Knob Mine in Macon County was first worked for sheet mica by Dr. Jim Lyle in about 1875. During this period, Yancey County had the Ray, Presnell and John Allen; Mitchell County had the Sink Hole and Cloudland; Avery County had not been formed yet; Lincoln County had the Jack Thomas Baxter; and Macon

County had the Mill Knob. Watauga County had Cranberry, so they did not need a mica mine. Cranberry is now located in Avery County. Capitol Mining Company was probably the last to work the Mill Knob in the mid-'50s.

• Shepherd Knob Mine, located on Bench Mountain just north of Caler Fork of Cowee Creek in Macon County, was a major scrap mica producer. This mine was being operated in the mid-'50s by Macon Mica Company.

• Lyle Knob was worked primarily for sheet mica and feldspar. Several pegmatites were worked at this location. In 1943, National Mica Company mined for scrap mica, as did Mica Products Incorporated in 1947.

• Chalk Hill Mica Mine, located on the lower slopes of Trimont Ridge in Macon County, was a limited producer of high-grade sheet and scrap mica. A.W. Reid built a scrap-processing plant on the Chalk Hill Mica Mine property in the early 1930s. Legal problems caused the plant and mine to be closed shortly thereafter.

• The Jack Thomas Baxter Mine, located in the southwest corner of Lincoln County, was one of the oldest mines in the Shelby Pegmatite District. It was worked for sheet mica prior to 1870. In 1947 and 1948, F.B. Hendrick worked it for scrap. The mine was an open pit and a major producer of scrap mica. After the deposit was depleted, it was back-filled.

• Some of the sheet mica producers of Cleveland County were: The Foster, The Bess, The Mull, The Baxter Girls, The Self, Indiantown and The Mauney. The Autrey-Robinson deposit was located on the north side of Bailey Mountain near Celo in Yancey County. The pegmatite and alaskite bodies, located on Shanty Ridge, have been mined for sheet mica, but as of 1953 the scrap mica had not been mined.

• The Bailey scrap mica deposit, located east of Penland in Mitchell County, was worked for clay and mica as a by-product since 1905 by Harris Clay and later by Carolina China Clay. Mining ceased at this location about 1942. There is still estimated to be between three and four million tons of ore left in this body of high-grade alaskite and kaolin.

• The Blue Rock Mine located off Blue Rock Road, 0.75 miles

west of Blue Rock Church, has been mined for sheet mica on and off for several years, presumably by the Newdale Mica Company, who owned the property. Several pegmatites of this mine had been mined by open pit and shaft.

• The Bowditch deposit located in Yancey County, one mile southwest of Bowditch, was worked for punch, sheet and scrap. It was located on the Blue Ridge Mining Company property.

• The Butler Gap Mine, located on the Ed Young Road east of Micaville, was mined in the early 1950s by Southeastern Mica Company for scrap mica. The ore was hauled to their processing plant located near Crabtree Creek in Mitchell County.

• Cox Knob Mine, located on Cox Knob 2.75 miles east of Micaville, was full of schist and returned only a marginal profit. The Cox was mined during the Depression at a time when most mines were closed. A man named Roland fell to his death there in the 1930s.

• The Crabtree Creek deposit in Mitchell County was mined for kaolin by Harris Clay. The mica was sold as a by-product.

• The DeWeld Mine was located 1.6 miles northeast of Celo in Yancey County on the north slope of Bailey Mountain. This alaskite body contained close to 500,000 tons of ore. Most of it probably is still there. In 1949, Asheville Mica Company started mining scrap at this location. The ore was mined hydraulically, washed over a mud screen, loaded on trucks and hauled to the processing plant located 1.5 miles to the south. Remember when South Toe was a river of mud? The DeWeld was one of the mines that caused that. In 1950, DeWeld Mica Company erected a concentrating plant close to the mine. This was one of the last, if not the last, jig mine to close. This was an efficient and cost-effective way to extract the mica, but the pollution cost to streams was just too great.

• North of the DeWeld Mine was the Ed Edge deposit, 3.3 miles east of Micaville on the Blue Rock Road. This deposit consisted of several pegmatites and was worked for both sheet and scrap mica. Beautiful emerald green blades of kyanite could be found in this area before it was filled in and seeded with grass.

• The Fawn Knob Mine was located 2.7 miles southeast of Micaville and 0.3 miles east of Blue Rock Road. Newdale Mica mined this deposit in the 1950s.

• The Theodore Freeman deposit was on Double Island Road, 2.8 miles northeast of Micaville. This mine was on Mr. Freeman's and Carolina Mineral Company's property. The estimated amount of ore that could be mined from this location was 350,000 tons containing nine to ten percent mica.

• The Gusher Knob and Brush Creek clay deposits in Avery County are well documented. Since 1937, they were owned and mined by Carolina Kaolin and Kaolin Incorporated. Clay was primary and mica was sold as a by-product.

• The Long Branch Mine, located at Newdale, was another clay mine operated by Harris Clay. This mine contained an estimated 1,600,000 tons of high-grade alaskite.

• The Jimmy Cut Mine was located on property leased to Jimmy Mayberry. The mine was on lower Browns Creek near Celo and about 1,000 feet from South Toe River. The Jimmy Cut produced a large amount of sheet mica. It appears the real wealth of this mine was in the clay, feldspar and scrap mica. It has been estimated there was close to 1,000,000 tons of high-grade, clean ore in the mine.

• The Micaville scrap mica deposit produced more scrap mica than any other mine in the Spruce Pine Pegmatite District up until 1951. For many years this deposit supplied ore to keep three scrap mica plants busy. US 19 E cuts through this deposit five tenths mile east of Micaville. The main deposit was on the south side of the road.

• The Newdale Scrap Mine was worked for several years for sheet mica. Later, it was worked for scrap by Newdale Mica Company and Southern Mica Company. Southern Mica had a plant close to the property. This mine was located on the ridge above Long Branch.

• English Creek in the Spruce Pine area was owned and mined at one time or another by Harris Clay, Newdale Mica or the Whitehall Company. This deposit was estimated to contain between four and five million tons of ore; Graveyard Creek contained between four and five hundred thousand tons of kaolin and alaskite; and Silver Run Creek was estimated to contain over one and one-half million tons of hard feldspar and alaskite. The mica content was between eleven and fifteen percent.

• Grassy Creek contained three kaolin mines that were owned and mined by William Wiseman. Kaolin was primary, and sheet and scrap mica were secondary. The sheet mica was the beautiful green, extra heavy mica sometimes found in the area.

• Sullins Creek was another Harris Clay operation. This deposit contained an estimated 1,200,000 tons of ore with mica content of seventeen percent.

• Three Mile Creek was mined for sheet mica as well as kaolin and scrap.

• The first scrap mica concentrating plant in Lincoln County was erected by the Victor Mica Company on the farm of John Peeler in 1943. For some reason, this plant was never used.

• In 1947, F.B. Hendricks built a washer plant in Lincoln County on the property of Jack Baxter. This plant was the real beginning of the Shelby District scrap mica industry. Later, the Kings Mountain Mica Company of Cleveland County built the state's largest and most modern concentrating plant.

• The Bun Patterson deposit of Kings Mountain has been mined by F.B. Hendricks and the Kings Mountain Mica Company. A drag line was used in an open pit. The pegmatite contained plagioclase, feldspar, quartz, muscovite, potash feldspar, biotite, garnet, granite, mica, gneiss and schist. Some halloysite clay stringers were found. The mica was of excellent quality and the scrap was best suited for wet grinding.

• The Charlie Moss deposit was in Cleveland County and as of 1955, had not been worked extensively. Spodumene has been mined in Cleveland County at several locations. One was on Kings Creek in the 1940s by Solway Processing Company of Syracuse New York.

Other deposits of scrap mica in the Spruce Pine pegmatite area include: Nichols-Grindstaff, Phipps Branch, mined by Asheville Mica; Robinson-Brewer, mined by Newdale Mica; Robinson Dairy, mined by Harris Clay; S.M. Edge, mined for sheet and scrap by Newdale Mica; Sparks-Robinson, first mined for sheet mica and later by Harris Clay, estimated to contain 100,000 tons of ore; Briggs-Woody deposit, located east of Celo; Burleson deposit on Fawn Mountain, southeast of Micaville; and Burnsville Mica Company deposit on Blue Rock Road. Burnsville Mica operated a concentrating plant at this site during the 1950s.

Domestic Mica Buying Policy

Mica today does not seem all that important but before substitutes were found, it was critical to our national defense and development. War machines could not have been built without mica. Mica was so critical that Hitler assigned some of his top scientists to develop a synthetic variety. Fortunately for the world, this was not an easy thing to do and the war was about over before synthetic mica was ready for use.

It seems that during World War II, some people wanted the government to buy India mica. Colonial Mica was the government agency responsible for setting the standards and buying policy for domestic mica. Another agency of the government was responsible for the purchase of foreign mica.

The industry had used and tested domestic mica and agreed it was of excellent quality. The green variety of mica found in the Spruce Pine area was tested and rated as excellent quality. This was not good enough for Colonial and they adopted the British-India specification as the sole buying standard. It was understandable and predictable when domestic miners and investors became upset because very little of the domestic mica could meet those specifications. Large volumes of this mica could be found in British-owned mines in India. Manufacturers who did not make war materials purchased enough domestic sheet mica to keep the price up. The industry felt that importing so much cheap mica kept the price of domestic mica well below its potential. There was an obvious problem and it had to be corrected.

In November 1944, Avery County educator and miner George Bowman called for a meeting of all area mica miners. Within a few days, Washington notified many large mica firms to make records available and be prepared to explain dealings. The legal process began. By the spring of 1945, many large mica companies were fined heavily for breaking antitrust laws. Apparently things were not going well with Colonial. Without notice, Colonial had all of its leased equipment returned to its Spruce Pine office. This caused a real shortage of equipment within the industry.

President Truman, then Senator Truman, got involved. The production board ordered the British-India specifications dropped. The government began to buy mica from local producers again, even the green variety. It is my personal opinion that the green mica was excluded from the list because Western North Carolina had so much of it and India had none. Industry had already rated it as a superior mica for electrical uses. If major manufacturers of war equipment specified green mica, this would have been a major problem for importers.

According to people I have talked to, the method of getting imported mica into the war materials stockpile disguised as domestic mica was simple and effective. Mica was purchased primarily from mine owners in India. The mica was shipped to a warehouse in Canada. Private trucks would pick up the mica in Canada and bring it into the United States. All of the shipping labels would be removed before delivery to the Spruce Pine depot. The rifters knew their job and mica. Most minerals, mica included, contain trace foreign minerals. The foreign minerals will vary from mine to mine. Trained rifters could see that. To get by that, the people involved in this project would talk for days prior to the arrival of the first shipment about new mica mines being worked in Maine. Some of the mica might be passed around to show what great quality the mica was. After the first truckload, the excitement subsided and new arrivals were treated as routine.

Talk about a sweetheart deal! Imagine being able to sell India's entire sheet mica production to the United States government at a huge per pound profit. However, this is only my opinion.

After Senator Truman became involved, enough evidence was assembled about wrongdoing in the mica industry to obtain a cease and desist consent decree. Heavy fines were paid by those involved. *The Tri-County News* dated December 13, 1951 carried a short update. At that time, the Department of Justice was still looking for a former official of the War Production Board who had a lot to do with forming government mica buying policies during World War II. They only wanted to question him at the time. This individual was tracked to Paris, France but seemed to have vanished.

When World War II ended, the mining activity began a gradual slowdown over a period of about five years. In 1951, things began to happen in the mining industry. Rumors began to circulate that the government was about to announce a new mica-buying program. Even before it was made official, mica miners began to clean out the old mines and get them ready. Water was being pumped out, decayed timbers removed and replaced with new ones.

Not only were mica miners getting ready, some of the larger feldspar plants expanded their production capacity. Local papers such as the *Tri-County Journal* in Spruce Pine had weekly articles describing the rapid expansion of the industry. This paper reported on August 2, 1951 that "Carolina Minerals Plant planned to increase the output of feldspar, ground mica and fine silica to its maximum capable production. Rated capacity of the new plant was twenty tons of raw material an hour. A plant of this type has to run continuously. There is little doubt that the yearly production of 84,000 tons will be met." In addition to the new plant, Carolina Minerals was currently operating the largest feldspar-producing plant in the world at Kona. The Kona plant was also the first in the world to use the froth flotation separation method.

To bring the new plant up to full production, close to one hundred thousand tons of raw alaskite would be needed annually. To meet this demand, the company purchased the old Hawkins Mine located about two miles from the plant.

This mine had been worked before by the Clinchfield Products Company. That company used an aerial tram to haul the raw alaskite from the mine to the railroad at Spruce Pine. Since it was so close to the processing plant, Carolina Minerals would use trucks. A truck could make a round trip every twenty minutes. Working a ten-hour day with a power shovel, one man could load 450 to 550 tons of material on the delivery trucks.

Today, the Hawkins Mine is being worked by Unimin Incorporated. The mine is being worked about the same as years gone by. Trucks are still being used to haul the spar from the mine to the plant. Also, the School House Mine at Ingalls is used to feed their major processing plant at Spruce Pine. The mining process itself has not changed much, but what has changed is how the spar is processed and used. The cleaning and separating process is a highly guarded secret. Some of the well-known new uses that put the Spruce Pine pegmatite minerals in such a high demand are fiber-optic phone lines, high-grade fiberglass, silicon chips, quartz halogen lamps and many other uses that do not require huge quantities.

It was estimated that in 1951, power equipment would be used to strip three and one-half million tons of earth that covered mineral deposits in the Spruce Pine area. That estimation was compiled from reports supplied by the twenty processing plants in the Spruce Pine area at the time.

Whenever I read about a study, advisory, evaluation board or panel being assembled, I get a little suspicious. First of all, you know these people are going to do very little for a lot of money. Second, I suspect the industry or project is in trouble. I began to see this more and more in the mica-mining industry during the 1950s.

One such committee of mica miners was formed to advise the National Production Authority. The subject discussed was the possibility of meeting national requirements for mica without depending on large imports from India. A couple of these committee members were well-known local people. It was of interest to me that most of the members were from New Jersey; Newport News, Virginia; Boston, Massachusetts; Brooklyn, New York; Schenectady, New York; and Chicago, Illinois. I wonder how many of these people knew anything about United States mica production and how many were in the mica import business. After all, the government program that had been such a problem for mica miners during World War II was beginning to surface again during the early years of the Korean War.

It was commonly believed that much had been learned during World War II. At the beginning of the Korean War, when the new policy was announced, most miners were shocked. The program announced that only ruby mica that met the British-India specifications would be purchased for strategic needs. There was such a flurry of anger and disbelief that the program was delayed. After several delays, the program was finally announced. By this time, the document itself was extremely long, complicated and changed almost daily.

When one change was announced, the editor of *The Tri-County News* received so many requests for help in deciphering the document, he ran a copy in the paper with an item-by-item explanation. It seems to me the later problems were caused by lack of knowledge, and not greed, as had been the case before.

After a lot of confusion and turmoil, it was obvious things had to change. In 1952, U.S. Flint of Crossnore was put in charge of the buying program. The entire domestic program was developed and administered from the Spruce Pine office. Mr. Flint was not a stranger to mica and the people of the area. He had mined mica for several years in the area. Some of his previous mining operations were the Birch, the Long Cut, Lincoln Park Number 3 and Bunker Hill. At the time of appointment he and his partner, C.J. Keller, were operating mica mines in Macon County. He gave those up.

By October 1953, the government was buying green mica again and, at least on the surface, everything was okay.

Another policy established in the early 1950s by the Defense Minerals Administration gave aid to miners of critical and strategic minerals. The government assistance would come in the form of contracts, where the government would pay from fifty to ninety percent of the cost of prospecting for new ore bodies of strategic minerals. Mica and beryl, which were among the most critical, were granted ninety percent participation by the government.

It was explained to me like this: When a miner applied for a loan or grant, a group of engineers would visit the site. An estimate would be made of the cost to remove topsoil, tunnel and build roads. A loan would be made up to ninety percent of the estimated cost. The people I knew who got loans received seventy-five percent of estimated cost. If you were a good miner, manager, and hard worker, you could complete the work for less than the estimated cost. It was unfortunate, but some miners had to find a good paying job to pay the debt.

For some reason, most of the miners did not know about this program for a year or longer after it was approved. Sam Phillips, Jr. of Wing brought it to the attention of local miners. Once it was made known, the applications poured in. Some of the first mining companies to apply for and receive loans were: Powder Mill Mining Company; Meadow Mine Mica Company; Charles Mica Company; Cook Mining Company; Brooks Beryllium (Swain County); Kelly Mine; Mitchell Creek Mica Miners (Upson County, Georgia); John Burke Mica Miners; Piedmont Minerals; Bess Gaston Mica Company; Gaston Strategic Mining Company; Earnest Mica Company; Trammell Mining Corporation; Hunter and Sullins Mica Company; Macon Mica #1, Franklin Developers; Macon Mica #2, Fred Cabe; Macon Mica #3, Lawrence Penland; Macon Mine #1, E.H. Zackery; Macon Mine #2, Mica Development; Macon Mine #3, Joe H. Ledbetter; Macon Mica #4, Harold Enloe; Macon Mica #5, F.A. Judson; Macon Mica #6, Non-Metallic Minerals Corporation; Olivine Products Corporation; Jackson Nickel; Henry Lee Robinson Mica; Wilkes Mica; Harold Enloe Mica; Macon Mica #7 and the Hitchcock Corporation (Hitchcock was mining talc at Murphy.)

It was not known at first that loans could not be granted to mines that produced green mica. Loans were at first granted, then denied, to the Cook, Charles and Meadow mines for that reason.

Mr. Phillips also helped in getting the government to reverse its policy on not buying green mica. Those loans and grants were extremely important to small mining operations. After the policy was reversed, loans were once again made.

By 1952, mica had come a long way since the days when it was used primarily as "isinglass" windows in the doors of coal-burning stoves. During World War II, it became an indispensable element of electronic devices. In fact, it became so important to our national defense, the government in 1952 set aside $40,000,000 to be used for the purchase of mica for the next three years. That was good news for mica miners. However, they could not rest easy. There was a danger someone in the importing business could get the rules changed and the government would only buy imported mica again.

One thing against domestic mica is that it costs more to mine. One thing in its favor is that during World War II, imported mica shipments were interrupted, causing a near panic. The United States could not afford to let that happen again. The $40,000,000 was for the purchase of domestic mica only.

In 1950, we were only producing 300 tons a year of strategic grade mica. This was fifteen percent of our defense needs. The $40,000,000 was not that much, but it would keep the mines open.

Western North Carolina & the War Years

One thing has become apparent during the compiling of this information. Miners did not stay in one place long. I suppose the major reason for changing locations was simply a person could not afford the expense of long-term mining if the mine was not producing. Just moving several tons of rock a day for nothing would cause me to change. If you were working for hourly wages, there were few if any companies which provided benefits to entice the workers to stay. Someone was always willing to make a really good miner a better offer. If mining for yourself, you were always looking for a better location.

The demand for minerals, especially mica, was a roller coaster that rose dramatically during times of war. The demand was up from 1915 to 1920. It was medium to low from 1920 to 1929 and practically nonexistent from 1929 to 1935. It began to pick up from 1935 to 1939. From 1939 to 1946, mica commanded a good price and you could sell all you could produce. By September 10, 1942 there were approximately one hundred and seventy-five major mica producing mines operating in Western North Carolina. Sixty to seventy of these were in Yancey County. Others were opening on a daily basis. Hundreds of private claims were being worked. Some of the major producers in Yancey County during 1942 were the Myra Gibbs, One, Two and Three, The Presnell, John Thomas Mines, Rose Branch, Ray Mines, Black Dixie, Lighted Rock, Big Ridge, Willie Shanty, Little Zeph, Bee Ridge, Carson Rock, Murphy Rock, Randolph, Howell, Abernathy, White Oak and Dutch Branch.

Western North Carolina miners and minerals were so important to the nation's defense that by law the miners were not required to take up arms. Miners could get a military service deferment, although most did not. There were three major mining corporations in Western North Carolina during the early war years: Capital Minerals of Washington, Meyers and Brown of New York and Industrial Minerals of Chicago and Asheville.

There was a slump from 1946 to 1952, but a good price from 1952 through 1955. From 1955 until 1997, price was low and demand was practically nonexistent. The price and demand for some of the other minerals mined during this time were less turbulent. With such an unstable market, mica miners sometimes were forced to change. Probably the reason for such a radical market was that the United States used most of the mica produced. Cheap labor in competitive countries also kept our exports down. The economy and military use controlled the demand.

During the war years, two products that Western North Carolina had were mica and pulpwood. Both industries had problems keeping up with demand. The feldspar industry thrived also. As usual, steel was scarce. To say spar was needed for the war effort in massive quantities would be a understatement. Just about every war machine had components manufactured from spar. Many things that were made from steel before the war, such as food storage containers, were now made from spar. Steel canning containers were replaced with glass. Cleaning compounds containing ground spar were in wide use. J.O. Stafford of New York built a plant named the Stafford Company beside the Feldspar Milling Company plant at Bowditch. The plant construction started in January 1942. It shipped the first carload of cleanser to the United States Navy on November 26, 1942. Normal production for the plant was sixteen thousand pounds over eight hours. Through 1944, three million pounds of this product were sold to the Navy. The Stafford Company's output was extremely small compared to the total production of spar.

On January 16-17, 1944, the Yancey Theater showed a film called "United States Army Salutes the Mica Industry."

The Mineral Kingdom

Former visitors to the area have described the Toe River Valley of Western North Carolina as the Mineral Kingdom. Actually, that description is close to the truth. Western North Carolina has more minerals per square mile than any other place on earth. In fact, of the more than 300 minerals known and identified, most can be found here. That is why every summer, mineral collectors from all over the world visit this area. There are mineral shows and swap meets in every county. Just about every family in the area was affected in some manner by the mining industry, the wagon builders, teamsters, railroaders, saddlers, mail carriers, geologists, mineralogists, blacksmiths, machinists and almost every profession and trade.

Many people have moved to Western North Carolina because of the jobs and investment opportunities minerals provide. The Presnells were a typical mining family. During the early 1820s, word came of the rich gold finds in the Carolinas. Thinking this was an excellent chance to better themselves, they picked up everything they owned and moved to Burke County, now Caldwell County. There, they mined the rivers and streams for gold, from the Catawba River, John River, Globe and Kings Creek District to high on the east slope of Grandfather Mountain.

Some of the Presnells decided mining wasn't for them and went on to other things. One was a suit maker in the town of Morganton; another had a farm that contained much of the land of present-day Morganton.

During that period, huge dredges were working the placer deposits on the Catawba River. Three thousand miners were working one stream in McDowell County in 1848. By 1850, hardly a mine could be found in the area. I do not know why the Presnells did not follow the rush to the new find in California. Some probably did, but most stayed in North Carolina. Some went to Union County, where there were large iron mines and some gold mines. Some went to present-day Alexander County, where gold and gemstones were being mined.

In newly formed Yancey County, it was believed by many that large deposits of gold would be found. Copper, iron and gemstone mining was already taking place in the area. At that time, Mitchell County and part of present-day Avery County were in Yancey County.

My great-great-grandfather Peter and his wife, Susan Teague Presnell, chose to come to Yancey County. John Presnell, probably Peter's brother, came along. John Presnell was the first owner of the Presnell Mica Mine in Yancey County.

History portrays people that followed the gold rush to be transients and undesirable. Of course, some did fit this description, but most did not. While in the Burke, Caldwell and Watauga County areas, the Presnells had homes, married, joined churches and voted in every election.

The state was growing and counties were changing but the miners led a fairly stable life. Shortly after moving to the mountains, the Civil War disrupted life as usual. Peter and Susan's oldest son, David, came to the mountains with the family. He went off to war, never to return. David died and was buried at Cumberland Gap, Kentucky. James, the next oldest, came to the mountains with the family. He also went to war and was last seen mortally wounded on the battlefield at Chickasaw Mountain, Georgia.

Great-grandfather Amos was too young to join the army during the war. There was very little mining being done, so he stayed behind and helped on the farm. By the end of 1872, Amos had married and needed to find a job. That should not have been a major problem, but it was. The economy should have been strong, but because some people had tried to take control of the gold market, there was a major slump in the economy.

Amos knew J.G. Heap, a tinsmith from Tennessee, was paying about five cents an hour for mica miners over at the Sink Hole Mine. He and his bride, Althea Riddle Presnell, moved from Brush Creek to Ledger, close to the Sink Hole Mine. I suspect he worked the mine.

Before 1880, Amos, his brother Harrison, nephew William, and Uncle John were working the Presnell Mine, located where the North and South Toe Rivers meet at Newdale. They worked the mine until about 1894. In 1883, the Presnell Mining Company sold two-thirds of its many holdings to J.K. Irby.

Amos's Uncle John owned the property on which the Presnell Mine was located for many years. In the 1890s, John leased the mine and the surrounding 400 acres of land to Jake Burleson for the purpose of mining. The mining profession was passed on down. My grandfather Cas was involved with mining all his life, as were my father Lonnie and his brothers. Many of my great-great-grandfather Peter's descendants became miners and settled in the Double Island, Newdale area of Yancey County.

Most of the miners of the early years were actually farmers during the summer and miners after the crops were laid by. Then, as today, carpenters go to where something is being built, miners go to where something is being mined.

In 1943, the *Tri-County News Journal* published an interview with John G. Phillips, age 93 years. With permission, I want to share some of that interview with you. At that time, Mr. Phillips was described as having an excellent memory. He could recall events that happened long ago and describe them as they progressed, hour by hour. Mr. Phillips had worked with mica pioneers such as Elisha Bouge Clapp, John G. Heap, Garrett Dewesse Ray, J.L. Rorison, Jake Burleson, R.T. Dent and W.B. Kester.

In 1943, it had been almost three quarters of a century since J.G. Heap, a native New Yorker, moved to Western North Carolina with wife, Anna Elizabeth. They came from Knoxville, Tennessee to be the first to mine mica on a large scale. Mr. Heap needed someone to prepare mica from local mines for shipment to market. This sheet mica was to be used in the fronts of hard-coal-burning stoves that furnished heat for the well-to-do families living near the anthracite fields of eastern Pennsylvania. Mr. John Phillips, a young fellow at the time, landed the job.

Mr. Heap was partners in a hardware business back in Knoxville with E.B. Clapp. Heap and Clapp formed a partnership in the mica business. Heap, a native of Massachusetts, bought Clapp's interest after his early death.

Before long, another person showed up on the scene who would become a mica pioneer. This was a stove manufacturer from Philadelphia named J.L. Rorison. Rorison was in Western North Carolina to purchase mica directly from the miners for use in his stoves. Once here, he commenced the task of finding the best man for the job. He made several contacts and asked a lot of people around Bakersville where to find an honest man who knew how to buy and prepare mica.

Apparently John Phillips had earned a good reputation for himself. Rorison sought out this 21-year-old and put him to work. Phillips displayed his abilities so well that before long he was in charge of all of Rorison mica activities in Western North Carolina. For more than fifteen years, Phillips bought mica for Rorison, cut it to pattern specification and shipped the finished product north.

During those years, Phillips had to contend with conditions that would now seem almost impossible. During the 1870s, John Phillips constantly covered the mines of three counties on horseback. There were practically no roads. Population was scant and outside markets for farm products was limited largely to what could be driven off on foot. The nearest railroad was at Johnson City. The road to Johnson City went over Iron Mountain, which four horses could negotiate with a wagon only a few months of the year. During the rest of the year, pack horses were used. The railroad had not been extended from Marion to Asheville, and rail service at Marion was limited. Phillips knew the mica must be delivered so he used whatever transportation was at hand. Sometimes he sent it by pack horse to Johnson City or from the nearest express station, which was located at Salisbury. Getting money into the area to pay the people Phillips employed was extremely risky business. Rorison Operations were being carried on in a country that had been almost a no-man's-land during the Civil War, which had ended only a short time before. Robberies were common and murders were frequent. Travelers rarely went over Iron Mountain alone and none would risk carrying large sums of money. Anyone known to be carrying cash and attempting to cross the mountain was taking a big chance. There was a good chance you and your money would disappear.

Large sums of money were often sent to John Phillips. He had to get the money from Johnson City to Bakersville. He hired his brother, Jim, to do that job. Jim was a big man. He would not start a fight, but he would not back down from anyone. It seems Jim's strategy was not to slip past places where thugs were likely to be, but to stop and replenish his drinking supply. John Phillips had several chances to earn big bucks from the mining industry. At one time he sold a mine for $1,500, which later produced more than that per week. John worked for the mining industry for several years and then returned to farming, where he spent many more years. John had no regrets.

Mineral Rights

Registered mineral rights can be found at the Register of Deeds office in a book called *Record of Conveyance of Sub-Surface Rights*. If you do not know who has the rights to mine the minerals from your land, you might want to look there. Someone has those rights and it might not be you. For many years, if someone owned the mineral rights on a piece of property, those rights remained in effect even though the property owner changed. This is still true, but today most mineral rights revert to the property owners.

The law was changed to protect the property owners if the mineral-rights holders did not update their records. If you decide to check out your property, I warn you to be prepared to spend a good deal of time. You might be lucky and find what you are looking for quickly. You might realize that you are enjoying what you are reading and continue to do so.

While looking up mineral rights in Yancey County, I saw information on a parcel of land my great-great-uncle John Worth Wiseman purchased in 1836. John was killed in the Civil War.

I saw other names like Tillman Blalock. Tillman is a historical figure and great-grandfather to the Blalocks Mining in the area. Most property owners are more than happy for large mining companies to own the mineral rights on their property. If the minerals are mined, the property owner gets a percentage of what is sold. To file a claim to mineral rights, you probably will need an attorney.[1]

---

[1]The state law that covers this subject is GSI-42, GSI-42.1 and GSI-42.9.

Pioneer Mining Families

From the first day I commenced this project, I wanted to talk to some real pioneers of the mining industry in the area. So far, I have talked to a few but their memory just wasn't what it was at one time. Whenever I spoke with a miner, I would ask if he knew anyone still alive who still had a good memory in this category. Someone gave me two names: 101-year-old Beverly Kester and Mrs. Roy (R.B.) Dent, who were both alive and well. Both of these women lived a short driving distance from Burnsville.

When I heard those names, I could not believe what I was hearing. Here were two people that were documented pioneers of the ground-mica industry. If you want to go back in time, I cannot think of a better way than to talk with someone who was there.

On November 2, 1993, I visited with Beverly Kester and her memory was sharp as a tack. I found her sitting quietly, with not a hair out of place. This definitely was a lady of distinction. Her 101 years had indeed been kind to her. I had to speak a little louder than normal and had a little trouble as I adjusted the volume.

She commenced to tell me her story. She told me her husband, W.B. Kester, lived in Pennsylvania as a young man and had gotten involved in the mica industry. W.B. heard of the mineral boom that was taking place in Western North Carolina and he moved here shortly after the turn of the century.

Not long after coming to the area, W.B. helped build one of the first mica grinding plants in the area. The company was the English

Mica Company. The officers were T.A. English of Spruce Pine, Walter M. Yeager, Robert R. Dent and David A. Teslar of Williamsport, Pennsylvania. Construction was started in November 1908. The shipments of ground mica started in the spring of 1909. W.B. was involved with mica and mining until he sold out to Ray Dent. The business prospered until the stock market crashed in 1929.

The English Mica Company, as well as many other businesses, was forced to make changes in the late 1920s and early 1930s. In May of 1929, J.B. Preston was general manager of the company when it was forced to make major changes. Almost ten years later in 1937, the business reorganized and went back to full production.

Beverly Mae met W.B. at Spruce Pine and married him January 18, 1911. Mrs. Kester said sometimes she forgets she is back in Spruce Pine, just across the river from where she was raised. Her family, the Phillips, had a farm along the river where the railroad is now. Her father built the first hotel in Spruce Pine and named it the Phillips.

I knew when I talked to this 101-year-old lady of distinction was a moment in my life I would not forget anytime soon. I could tell this was a lady that did not just sit back and let the world pass her by. However, her hearing was not good and although she seemed to enjoy the conversation, I felt uncomfortable sitting there yelling at her. I thanked her and promised I would return for another talk. I truly hope I get to keep that promise.

Amos Presnell

On November 21, 1992, I visited with my uncle Amos Presnell and Amos' wife, Pearl, at their home on Bolens Creek near Burnsville. Amos was raised in a family that mined for a living and was a miner himself from the mid-'30s to the mid-'50s.

After the price of mica dropped until mining was no longer profitable, Amos became one of Yancey County's most sought-after rock masons. Pearl, who worked for several years grading and cutting mica, is now well known for her beautiful handcrafted dolls and quilts.

One of the first mines Amos worked at was the Stanley Mine. Uncle Stanley came in late one evening and showed Uncle Herman and Amos a large book of mica he had found and told them he would need some help, if they were interested. Herman apparently was expecting a joke to be pulled on him. He said, "Sure, I bet you need some help; just what would you take for half interest in this mine?" Stanley offered half interest for Herman's black mule. Herman was not about to go for that trade.

Early the next morning, Stanley and Amos were on location digging hard. Amos dug down about shoulder deep in one hole and Stanley in the other. Amos was about to holler "calf rope" when Stanley came out with a book of beautiful red mica about the size of both hands. Amos came out of where he was digging and into where Stanley was. Amos still had not found anything when Stanley came out with a book even better than the first. They switched holes again. This pattern continued until late afternoon. The mica they found was put behind a large log. Herman showed up, saw these large holes, no mica, and had a good chuckle. Stanley told him to go over and look beside the log. Right away, Herman wanted to trade that mule, but "no deal." Stanley had already found enough to make a claim. At that time, you got a claim signed by the property owner and you were in business. The claim was no more than an agreement or contract between you and the property owner, protecting both parties. In early years, much of the time it was a verbal contract. That had changed by the late 1930s. Royalties on mica were 12.5 percent off the top; for spar, it was fifty cents per ton. Royalty was compensation to the land owner.

Amos had seen mica on the ground here before, but since it was close to the Silvers, which was active since 1902, he thought that was the origin. Stanley got the lease and was ready to go. He offered Amos ten cents per hour for sure, and fifteen cents if possible to come and help work the mine. He never got less than fifteen cents per hour. Before

Amos Presnell retired from mining in 1980, but he still likes to prospect. That's a specimen-collecting bag he's got strapped around his shoulder.

roads were built to the mine and machinery could be brought in, all drilling was done by hand. Amos and Herman contracted to drill three holes five feet deep per day for $1.50. If they were in soft rock, the work was easy and fast. If they were in hard rock, such as quartz, they would have to work into the night. At that time mica sold by the square inch and weight. The more good square inches per sheet of mica, the more per pound.

The price and quality specifications were constantly changing. For instance, *The Yancey Citizen* printed price and/or quality specification changes on March 20, 1952, April 3, 1952 and September 4,

1952. These articles were quite long. When mica sold for $5 a pound the miners got more money for their mica than when it went for more than $70 a pound. The reason was that some inclusions were acceptable, such as smudge of blue on green seen on some mica if you looked closely. At the high price, quality standards were high and strict. All inclusions had to be cut away and sold as scrap. Scrap sold for about $30 per ton. When the government supported the price of mica, the miners thought this would help, but it seems to have had the opposite effect.

I know that money changes people and things but how could it affect electrons? Before the price increase, this mica seems to have worked perfectly as a thermal and electrical insulator. I must have fallen asleep during the physics and economics class. I know there was no way anyone would take advantage of the working miner who put food on the family table by the sweat of his brow, or take advantage of the government (citizens), especially during the time of a national crisis. It must be true that money can modify behavior of anything, even electrons.

One day, Amos and Dad were working at the back of the Stanley Mine. The quantity of mica had slowed to a trickle. Basically, they were just drilling, blasting and removing the muck with little to show for it. Stanley came in, looked the situation over, told them to stop what they were doing, bring their equipment and follow him. He went to a location near the front of the mine. There was a little mica showing but it did not look like much. They drilled and shot. After the smoke cleared they went back in expecting to only find a mess to clean up. Instead it looked like someone had backed in a truck loaded with mica and dumped it. It was apparent that Stanley was either extremely good or extremely lucky. Amos believes it was the first.

From there the vein went east and laid flat like a coal vein, sedimentary. This was probably the vein that produced the clear spar, garnet and apatite that can be found in the dump today. After several years, the yield dropped until it was not profitable. After closing for awhile, Stanley, Amos, Latt Fox and Vernie Wilson made an unsuccessful attempt to relocate the vein. The Stanley deposit was thought to be depleted but the mica quality had been so good that if the old vein or a new one could be located, the expense would be worth it. A large dozer was contracted to push away the topsoil. The old mine works were covered over. No new vein was located.

My grandfather, Cas Presnell, built a mica trimming and grading house next to his home on Bolens Creek. He hired people to process the mica mined by Dad, Herman, Stanley, Amos and other local miners.

Probably the next mine Amos worked was the Kyanite Mine on Bill Allen Branch. When he asked the foreman for a job, the foreman said, "Do you know how to use a hammer?" Amos replied, "Sure, I have operated on some." The man said, "I'm not talking about a jackhammer" and handed him a sixteen-pound sledge, saying, "go to work."

For the first couple of weeks he broke rock with a hammer. After that he operated a drill. They would drill deep holes far apart, using low powdered twenty percent dynamite to blast off large chunks. Amos never knew why this method was used. Once it was blasted off, ten to fifteen men would use sixteen-pound hammers to break the rock and remove the kyanite. From there it would go into the processing plant, which was on location. A fellow named Matson was the operations manager. Swinging a sixteen-pound hammer or hanging on the side of the cliff ten hours a day was hard work, but if you did not want to, you did not have to, because there were plenty of people waiting to take your job. When Amos quit that job, his steel carrier got the jackhammer job. It was not long before that man fell to his death.

After the Kyanite, Amos went to work with Lee Ray and Rex Yelton at Isom Mine on Cattail Creek near Pensacola. Amos remembered that Elzie Rice also worked there. Elzie was already up in years and his bones were twisted by arthritis but he continued to work. Charles Wilson was also working there as the compressor operator. Most of the time during that period, the compressor was not any one person's responsibility but when Charles was there, the compressor was far below the mine. Walt Riddle was hoist operator. At one time, Amos had the job of lowering the rail car that hauled the mica down the mountain. The full car would go down one set of tracks and pull the empty car back up another set of tracks. The empty car was not heavy enough to keep the full car from running away, so Amos tied a huge chunk of iron to the cars. The brakes, along with the iron, would cause sparks to shoot into the night darkness that could be seen for miles.

The Isom was found in the late 1800s by Isom Silvers and had produced a large quantity of mica, including several books weighing up to 800 pounds. This was in the early 1940s. The mine was a vertical shaft with a large opening which tapered down quite small, with a cover over the opening. There was a trap door in the cover. The muck bucket would be lifted through the door, then the door would fall shut to prevent someone from falling through. When the bucket was lowered, it would dump into a waiting muck car that was mounted on tracks. The muck car would then be moved to the edge of the muck pile and dumped. Two rail tracks were laid down the mountain to the road. The top car would be loaded with mica. When let down it would pull up the empty car. The shaft went straight down for fifty feet and then turned slightly to the east. To keep the bucket from turning over on the way down, wooden skids were mounted to the wall. Amos only worked here for a short period of time until Uncle Sam needed him in Europe.

Amos was assigned to the Army's First Infantry Division, First Battalion. After fighting across Europe he wound up next to the Rhine River in Germany. A chunk of hot shrapnel passed through his body close to the heart. He stayed at a field hospital there until he could be moved. From there he was shipped to hospitals in France, England, Belgium and finally back to a hospital in the States for a short stay. The doctor told him to take it easy until he got his strength back. In those days you did not expect to be pampered nor could you afford to pamper yourself. Amos got home Thursday or Friday and by Monday morning he was back on the job at the Isom Mine.

The first day's work included two climbs out of the mine. His leg muscles would knot and cramp, but this did not stop him. Paul Yelton was job foreman at the time. He gave Amos the hoist operator's job. This continued on for awhile; then the mine was temporarily closed. The war had ended and price and demand for mica had dropped. Joe Goodin, Walt Lockridge and Charles Proffit were also involved with that operation.

Forty years after the last miner left, the Isom still blows its cold, wet breath.

Early in 1952, the Yancey Miner's Association decided to work the Isom again, headed by Joe Godfrey. Several other old mines were re-opened in Yancey County in 1952, including the Green Mountain on Shoal Creek and the Griffith at Windom. The March 20, 1952 issue of *The Yancey Record* reported that the government would start buying mica. Depots would be built in Spruce Pine, North Carolina; Keene, New Hampshire; and Custer, South Dakota.

The top vertical shaft of the Isom was full of water and not suitable for working. Amos was hired to blast a horizontal service shaft approximately 525 feet to intersect with the top vertical shaft. He started the job, left for awhile, then came back. There was some thought that the millions of gallons of water in the top shaft might break through into the bottom shaft with undesirable results. Amos was drilling to blast when they broke through. The rock held, so they drilled extra holes and waited for the water to drain before the rock was removed. When they did this, it created a minor problem. It created such a draft you could not put on enough clothes to stay warm and do the work. Eventually doors were built to block the draft. They moved a hoist to the back of the tunnel and started down.

They had not gone far when they found mica. They had soon swamped the cutters and graders at Micaville and a warehouse was found to store the mica until the rifters could catch up.

One time Amos shot three ten-foot holes. The rock came off as one large chunk. He started to drill and shoot again but everywhere he started, he would hit mica. Finally he drilled anyway and blasted. When he blasted, the hoist was broken so they had to sack the mica and get it out of the way so they could continue. There were seventy sacks and several blocks too large to sack. There were probably ninety sacks in all from that one shot.

There was beautiful blue-green microline spar in the Isom. I mentioned this to Amos. He said if you turned the lights off in the mine, after your eyes adjusted you could see a faint green glow. He picked some up and took it out into the sunlight to see just what was glowing in the dark. Apparently this mineral can be phosphorescent—or his eyes could have been playing tricks.

During this period, a lot of mica was removed from the mine, including some large books. Amos remembered one book that was longer than a full-grown pry bar. Finally the vein narrowed to nothing. Amos drilled sixteen-foot deep holes all over, but was not able to locate the vein. Soon the mine was closed again. Yates and Mark Bennett got a lease on the mine. Dad took a crew in. The crew I remember was Bill Miller, Bassey Bennett, Earl Ogle, Ed Calloway, Robert Rathbone, Lee Buchanan and a few others. This job ended a mining career that had lasted over thirty years for Dad.

After this crew left, Ken Blalock and his brother John went back and robbed the shaft. Amos got permission, went back and removed some large books of mica that had been left. After a long history this mine was closed, probably forever.

Amos mined very little at the Ray Mine. He remembered the time the truck came up to deliver dynamite. This was a one-ton truck, loaded, with chains on the tires. Going up the hill, a case fell off. The truck could not make it up the hill so he backed up to get another start, backing over the dynamite. On the next try, the spinning tires and chains threw the dynamite everywhere. The nearby miners were no longer nearby. They were long gone. The dynamite did not explode.

Before Amos was old enough to mine, he would go down to the Ray Mine with Dad. When Dad would roll out a wheelbarrow of muck, he would show Amos which rock to break if he wanted a beryl crystal. He would break it and, sure enough, most of the time one would be in there.

One time Dad and Amos were trying to drill a hole in a small passage with not enough room to cuss a cat without getting hair in your mouth. Dad was wearing a face mask, the type with the large canister filter on the front. He got irritated and grabbed the mask by the filter to remove it. The elastic straps stretched out to about arm's length when his finger slipped. The next time he got it off.

One time Amos had a job offer in Connecticut. The offer sounded good, so he packed up and headed north. When he reported for work, things did not look all that good. There was a gasoline driven water pump operating in the bottom of the shaft. Blue smoke was billowing from the top of the shaft. After looking at the equipment and the situation, he knew this was not for him. It was a death trap. But since he was already there, he decided to look a little closer. He started down the ladder. When he got close enough to see the men at the bottom, it was obvious there was a problem. Some of the men were lying flat down, while some were crawling around on hands and knees. They had taken the hoist cable from the bucket and connected it to something else. One man tied a small electrical cable around his body and called for Amos to pull him up. Amos knew this would not work. He instructed the man to get the hoist cable loose and connect it to the bucket and get in. One man started helping the other into the bucket. The man put the cable on the bucket, slipped the clamp in place and signaled to be lifted before the clamp was tight. The bend in the cable was all that was holding all that weight. Amos knew there was going to be a disaster. As the bucket passed him, the man with the wrench was steadily working on those nuts. They made it out and, with a little fresh air, they were alright. It was not long before Amos loaded his equipment and left.

Once, when Dad and Amos were mining the Silver Mica Mine, they knew there was one large rock overhead that was cracked. When they got time, they were going to cut a support and put it in place. One day Amos was working close to that location when Dad shouted a warning. Amos thought the large rock was falling. That rock had weighed several tons. He would not have had a chance for survival. The one that had fallen was about the size of two hands. He started running down the muck car track. The rock had fallen from the entrance. It hit him at the base of the skull on the back of the head. Dad checked him, thought he was dead and went outside for help. When he got back, Amos was trying to get up. Dad helped him up and started to the doctor's office. Amos did not know anything, but with help he could walk. The doctor put something on his head to prevent infection and told him to pay the lady at the desk. Like I said, in those days you were not pampered. After a couple of days, he began to get his senses back. For a while he could recognize a face, but could not put a name to it. After a week or two, that all came back. He still has a depression where the rock hit him. Obviously his skull was cracked. Amos thinks the hat he was wearing saved his life. It was made of thick leather, heavy enough to deflect and absorb some of the blow. Not much, but maybe just enough.

Shelby Hall, Tom Edge, Lee Hilliard, Pete Coletta and Dad bought a lease on the Balsam Mine. Dad was the only owner that also was working the mine. He got a share of the profits and a salary. Dad talked Amos into helping him at least for a couple of weeks. Amos knew this was a hard mine to work. It was a vertical shaft about 500 feet deep and shaped a little like a corkscrew.

Since it was last mined, it had filled with water. The first job was to get the water out. At first they pumped, using a pneumatic-operated pump. When the distance overcame the pump's ability, they used the hoist and a 100-gallon bucket to dip the water out. This proved to be too slow. Next they started connecting pumps in line. This method worked satisfactorily. Dad told me he had worked this mine fifteen years earlier and had used the carbon flame of a carbide light to write his name on the wall. When the water was out, he found his name there just as he had left it.

Amos was hired to operate the hoist. Lunch time came and there was not a cook, so he decided he would do it. He went to the cook shack. There was not much food there for him to prepare; just enough corn meal to bake a cake of bread about as thick as a shoe sole, and it turned out about as tough. He managed to get a few other odds and ends together. However, it was not nearly enough. After the meal, one of the men got Dad off to the side and Amos heard him ask if that man was hired to be the cook. Dad told him no, that Amos would do whatever needed doing. Dad asked him if he wanted to be the cook. The man made it real clear he did not want the job; all he wanted to know was if Amos was going to be the cook.

Amos said sometimes in the winter it would rain and freeze an inch thick on the ladder that went down into the mine. Dad would climb down, chipping off the ice one rung at a time. Standing on ice with nothing but 500 feet of air to break your fall would definitely wake you up. One day an inspector showed up. Amos escorted him down into the mine, stopping at the first heading and leaving him there. Amos went back up to operate the hoist. The bucket they were using was one-inch thick cast. When it struck a rock, it would bong like a large bell. Amos got the signal to pull. He knew the inspector at the time was not in harm's way, so he pulled it up. Due to the corkscrew shape of the mine, the bucket made a horrendous sound all the way out. To lower the bucket, he had to let it free fall or it would get lodged and tumble end over end.

The inspector below had no way of knowing what was going on. One can only imagine what he must have been thinking. Something had happened to his light, so he had none. Amos would not pull the bucket again until he located the inspector, so he shouted from the top several times with no response. Amos had a carbide lamp, but no hat to connect it to so he carried it in his hand and started down. He got down part of the way and could hear the fellow calling, trying to get the attention of the miners at the bottom. Amos continued down the ladder. He had not gone far when his lamp slipped from his hand. It went by the inspector like a torch. Amos made it on down to where he was. Amos assured the inspector that he knew every rung on the ladder, to follow him and stay close and he would take him down to the bottom. When they got to the bottom, after a couple of minutes, Amos said he was going back to the top and pull the bucket. The inspector said, "If you do not mind, I'll follow you out." Dad was there and told him to come back and visit them from time to time. The inspector said, "Hell no! I won't be back!" Lonnie eventually sold his interest in the Balsam Mining Company. The mine was still producing "A" mica when it closed. It was just too difficult to work.

Another location Amos worked on was at Shelby. The mine was located close to the high school and railroads. The mica was found in a large quartz vein. The quartz was all broken up. The only tools needed were hammers and pry bars. The problem was water and it finally got to be more than the pumps could handle. People were complaining their wells were being drained. Amos and William Moody, along with others, worked that mine. After the water got to be more than they could handle, the mine was abandoned. Another group went in later and was able to control the water. A lot of mica was removed.

If roads were not built to the mine or gasoline-powered hoists were not available to remove the muck from the mine, the miners would build their own hoist. To do this, they would bury a large post in the ground and attach guy cables to the top. Around the post they would build a drum. Cable was wound around the drum. A long arm called a sweep was attached to the top of the drum. A horse was used to raise and lower the loads.

Amos told me that one time my father, Lonnie, and their brother Stanley were working the vertical shaft of the Shanty Mine. Amos was there but was not old enough to be of much help. Stan had built a mechanical hoist for lifting and lowering the muck bucket. Normally, a horse would be used to pull out the load but if they did not have a horse there, a couple of men could lift out about a thousand pounds of muck at a time. One day Lonnie was ready to go back into the mine, so he got into the bucket to be lowered to the bottom. Stanley's mind must have been on something else because he gave the sweep a hefty push and let it run free. That would be normal if the bucket was empty. Amos had climbed up and was lying on the sweep. He was going to ride it around just for the fun. After a couple of turns, it had gained enough speed until he was about to be sent flying through the woods. He began to yell at Stanley, telling him that Lonnie was in the bucket. Stanley realized what he had done and tried to stop the runaway hoist. It dragged and threw him all over the place, but before the muck bucket reached the bottom, Stanley had slowed it down to normal speed. Lonnie must have not known

Workers watch water pour from the vertical Isom mine shaft through the hole Amos Presnell had just drilled.

the danger he was in because a few minutes after reaching the bottom, they could hear him whistling and singing to himself as he worked.

Today, the timbers that were in the tops of the vertical shafts have decayed away. The tops of the mine shafts, probably not over twenty feet across at that time, have caved in to close to one hundred feet. The old mines resemble huge funnels. I would not recommend anyone unfamiliar with that area walking around at night.

Dad was not working the Deer Park Mine at Spruce Pine, but one afternoon during a visit he was deep within the mine. Outside, rocks rolled down a hill, knocking over a metal shed. The first thing Dad thought was that there had been a cave-in. Then he remembered he had not eaten breakfast that morning and thought if they were blocked in, he would be the first to starve to death. They were not blocked in.

The Flem Mine was not that deep but the air circulation was bad. When blasting, much of the oxygen in the work area is burned away but most of the time air circulation replenishes the oxygen by the time the miners are ready to return to work. At the Flem Rathbone, going in after an explosion was extremely dangerous. As in most vertical shaft mines, there was a ladder to the bottom. The miners preferred using the ladder in this mine to riding the bucket down. Most mornings there would be a four-foot-deep pool of water where the bucket would sit down. Of course, you had to get out where the bucket was. If you climbed down the ladder, chances were you would stay dry. Also, if you rode the bucket down, you had to push it from side to side to prevent it from becoming lodged. If it became lodged it could turn bottom-up, dumping you out head first. The cable used to lower the bucket would be slapping from wall to wall and could cause a rock to fall. If there was a miner in the bucket, he would be a perfect target. For that reason, Amos normally decided to use the ladder.

One morning he reached the bottom and found it dry where the ladder was, but the bucket was in chest-deep water. Amos was afraid the air might be bad so he took several deep breaths trying to determine if it would be okay. Other than the normal stale smell of sulfur, the air seemed okay. The use of birds for testing the air was common in coal mines but not in mica mines. The damp-flame method was used some, but today Amos would trust his nose and lungs. He skirted the water hole and made his way to the heading where they had been working. He was anxious to see what the last shot had produced. There were several nice books of mica scattered about. He decided to pick these up before starting the pumps to remove the water. The quality and amount of mica was exciting. While picking up the mica his vision became blurred, breathing became shallow, and his head began to throb. Now he became genuinely worried; there was little if any oxygen in the air. His first thought was to get into the bucket and ring for a pull. Amos went through a career change in a hurry. He no longer was a miner, he was a runner. He was not a runner for long. Remember the deep puddle of water? Amos was a swimmer. He made it to the bucket and climbed in, ready to signal, but hesitated. What if the bucket should hang up on the way out and dump him back to the bottom? His job as a button operator lasted less time than his running job had. Back into the water. Amos was a swimmer again, headed for the ladder. When resting on the ladder, he would wedge his legs between the wall and the ladder to prevent falling if he should become unconscious. He made it out and prepared to pump fresh air into the mine so he could become a miner again.

If you mention a mine to Amos, he can usually tell you when it was mined, who mined it and what they found. During the last few years, Amos told Wanda and me about many places we might find minerals of interest. He actually took us to one location where we found some high quality smoky quartz. This location was near the top of a steep, rough mountain. The walk did not seem to bother Amos. Wanda and I did not fare so well. Amos and Pearl are still active and it is a real treat to sit and talk to them.

Lonnie Lee Presnell

If there was only one thing I could say about my father, Lonnie Lee Presnell, it would probably be that he loved to mine and he was good at it. When the demand for mica dropped, he would do other things such as farm, cut pulpwood or work as a powder man on the Blue Ridge Parkway. He even spent a short hitch in the Navy, but when the demand for mica went up, he would come back to that. He once mined tungsten in Henderson, North Carolina, but his love was mica mining. Miners of clay, spar, asbestos knew what they were going to get per blast or scoop and there was no excitement. Lonnie studied minerals and geological formations until he understood them.

I know very little about my grandfather Cas Presnell's mining days but I bet Lonnie was there with him when he got old enough. If there was mica to be found, Dad could find it. He knew where and how to drill the holes to get the best results and do the least damage to the mica. Also if there was a job to be done, while others were trying to figure out how to do it, Dad would already have it completed. I have talked to a lot of miners who worked with Dad over the years and they all told me about the same thing.

Dad would work at a mine all week and many times spend his weekend prospecting. I remember one weekend Dad, brother Max and myself left grandfather's house on Bolens Creek and walked up the old road that follows the creek. Dad was raised in

Lonnie Presnell was a miner. He was proud of that.
This was the last mine he worked, the Isom.

those mountains and he knew every rock and tree. First, we passed by what I think was the Old Copper Mine. Dad explained that the old-timers said that mine was there when the first whites settled. We did not dig any there. A little further we began to find small digs where others had prospected before us. Dad would pick a spot and began shoveling out dirt, inspecting every book of mica. He would take the mica found and bury it next to a rock or tree where he could find it later. Today, we talk about crafts that are lost; add shoveling to the list. Those miners could move huge amounts of dirt and rock and make it look so easy. As we moved from prospect to prospect, the process would continue. There were some larger mines in the area but we would not stop at those. Someone probably already had the mineral rights or Dad knew it had already played out.

During the day, a pheasant began to use its broken wing act to lure us away from its nest. It worked with me and I began to try to catch it. It did not work with Dad; he went over to where a chestnut tree had fallen and came back with a hat full of fresh pheasant eggs. We found an old bucket a miner had discarded, built a fire and had boiled eggs with our lunch. We continued across the Moody Mountains and came out on Laurel Branch at Pensacola. When the Moodys moved to the mountain, they gave it their name. Now that they are dead, hardly a trace of their graves can be found.

Brother Haston worked a lot with Dad and went on many such trips with him. He said Dad had a small pile of mica hidden at every mica vein in those mountains. I remember one prospect at Murchison he worked which had nice blue spar. I would like to go back there some day.

When Lonnie worked for Mark and Yates Bennett at the Isom, he was job foreman. Occasionally when the crew knocked off for the day, he would continue working, sometimes through the night. During one of those times, he blasted out a book that weighed over 1,400 pounds. Normally, he would blast and then knock off. That would let the smoke settle before the workers were due to come back in. That evening, he went back in. When he saw the huge book of mica, he went back to the bunkhouse and got Bassey Bennett to help him get it out. They were not lucky enough to get it to the top in one piece. When they tried to move it, it came apart. That did not hurt the quality.

At one time or another, Dad mined every one of the Ray Mine shafts. He and Monroe Calloway were the first to mine the Little Ray. They were at a depth of about fifty feet when Dad received an eye injury. He never came back to the Little Ray even though it did turn out to be a good producer. It also produced some real gem aquamarine. Some of the crystals were large.

When Dad was working at the Ray Mines, he was trying mostly to locate new mica veins. The mica that was easy to locate and remove had been removed before he was born in 1906. He knew the Ray was a super pegmatite and there must be other rich dikes in the area. To locate them would require drilling many test holes and that would cost far more than he could afford.

Silicosis was not talked about much in those days but most professional hard-rock miners died from it. Dad was diagnosed as having silicosis and TB in 1952. Once the lungs were weakened by the illness, TB was sure to follow. Once this condition was described to me as a combination that could not be beat.

Lonnie had always been extremely active. During those days, people with active TB were quarantined. It was as though you were in prison and you were not treated much better. That must have been extremely demanding and degrading. There were no television or movies, female and male patients were segregated, your children could not visit you, you could not mail out packages and life seemed unfair.

A Steel Driving Man

In 1905, Carl McHone was born into a mining family living in Mitchell County. When he became strong enough to swing a hammer, he went to work in a mine, sinking steel. The methods changed over the years but Carl did not. Almost all of his working days were spent drilling holes for the powder man. In 1995, Carl was the oldest living drill man in North Carolina.

In the early years, when a hammer was the primary tool for driving steel, the shock would be transmitted through the handle to the user. To prevent this, Carl would hew the handle down until it was small and flexible except for the hand hold. Once he found the proper harmonic rhythm, the bounce of the hammer would work for him.

One time, Carl worked a mine between Spruce Pine and Bakersville called the Ray. I knew of the Ray at Burnsville but I had not heard of that one, at least by that name. When he worked there, the mine was one and one-tenth mile deep. It was primarily worked for spar but also produced a lot of good mica. The workers kept a kerosene-fueled lamp sitting on a ledge near the bottom of the mine. If the flame turned to what was called a "black damp," that meant there was very little oxygen left in the air and time for all the miners to get out.

Hoists to lower and raise material from the mine were set up at intervals from top to bottom. This was also the primary method used to get the workers in and out. If word came down that the next bucket would carry "fresh meat," workers would stay clear. "Fresh meat" meant a new workhand would be coming in for the first time. For whatever reason, the hoist operators liked to let the bucket free-fall when a new person was going down. I bet if you had any phobia such as close spaces, falling, heights, darkness, etc., you were cured by the time bottom was reached.

Carl worked many mines in the Mitchell County area, including the Deke. His grandfather, Zack McHone, sold the first mica from the Spruce Pine area.

David Norman of Snow Creek came into the mica mining industry late and only worked a few years as a miner. He is extremely knowledgeable about miners, mines and minerals in the area. David's father, Willard Norman, had worked all of his working years as a miner. David worked some at the Howell Mine on Mine Creek, an underground mine. The shaft went at an incline to a depth of around 700 feet. A couple of friends that worked with him were Grover McKinney, first shift hoist operator, and Clarence Howell, second shift hoist operator. The Howell was a good sheet-mica producer.

David also worked the main shaft of the Sink Hole Mine. That shaft was about 350 feet deep at the time. Close to David's home, Homer Silvers was working a mica mine. Homer was getting large books of mica and also large beryl crystals.

The Johnny Thomas Mine, close to David's house, was also a good producer. At one time, clay was mined near the head of Mine Creek and flumed to Kona. David remembers when part of the old flume line was still visible even though mining had ceased many years before.

Charles Wilson lived in the Roan Valley many years and operated a trout fish hatchery. During his childhood, he was quite familiar with the mining industry. Charlie was from a family of miners. His home was in the Micaville area. Before he was old enough to work in the mines with his father and grandfather, Charlie was buying scrap mica from the local mines and grading houses for one cent a pound and selling it in Spruce Pine for three cents a pound. Charlie was earning more money than the mine workers.

His grandfather was working the Goug Rock in 1936, when they had the big cave-in. Charlie's grandfather noticed a crack opening up in the wall near the top of the shaft which I believe was about 900 feet deep. Each day the crack would be a little wider. One night about 3 a.m., Charlie's grandparents felt the ground shake and heard a loud rumble. That section of the mine was never opened again.

Charlie has property today that borders the Old Asbestos Mine. He had relatives that also worked this mine. The mine was last worked by the Burlesons and closed in the 1960s due to lack of demand for asbestos.

Miners, Rifters & Cobbers

During World War II, there were approximately 2,200 miners in the Yancey, Mitchell and Avery County areas. There were approximately 1,500 people employed in sheeting mica. Sheeting and trimming mica was a specialized trade passed down from generation to generation. At first glance, it would appear that anyone could do this job but that is not the case. The success of the mica mines was totally dependent on the sheeter. The official name was rifter. This person could truly make or break the business. Most of the mica sheeters in the United States were located in the Toe River Valley area. They were paid by the hour. More than likely, the pay did not nearly match their worth.

Many investors got the mining fever and came here with a large bankroll and probably a shirt. Many had lost both by the time they left. Probably their downfall was not hiring experienced help. Good help was hard to find and expensive when you found it. Apparently, many investors were led to believe that anyone who could swing a hammer was a miner.

Western North Carolina had the minerals, and most of the time, the market was strong. All that was required was to get the mineral from the ground, processed and to the customer in a good, useable condition at a cost that would permit a profit for all. We had the experts who could do that. They had been miners and had worked in mine-related jobs as their fathers and their forefathers had done. Most of the early miners of this area had left the coal, copper and iron mines of the North and East to work the gold deposits of North Carolina. When that played out, they came to the mountains to work the iron, copper and gemstone mines.

When mica mining started, we not only had experienced miners, we had experts. By the time World War II came, we had several generations of mica miners and at least one generation of feldspar and clay miners who had worked local mines. I bet some of the people who left their bankroll here wish they had hired more of these people.

Top prices were paid only for large solid sheets of mica. Even if you found a good vein of mica, if you did not have a good drill and powder man, you probably were not going to break even. A good drill man knew how and where to put the holes. If the powder man did not know how to load the holes properly, either the holes would not pull at all, or would be left in large chunks, or the mica could be broken into scrap and possibly your equipment destroyed. The difference was, some mica brought $70 a pound and some brought $30 a ton.

After the blast, the muckers and cobbers came in. The cobbers' job was to separate the rock from mica. The muckers removed the debris and prepared for another cycle to begin.

Next came the splitters (called rifters) and trimmers. At a glance, the rifter could determine the color and grade.

All the imperfections were cut away and the mica was cut into straight-edge shapes. The only tool needed was a razor-sharp knife. This was done on a white table with bright lights. Most rifters could look at a book of mica and identify the mine it came from.

Within one week in July 1952, miners removed 15,000 pounds of good-grade mica from the Isom. Lonnie Presnell, with the help of Bassey Bennett, removed one block that weighed 1,456 pounds. Mica from that lot sold for an average of $25 per pound. Pictures of the mica were shown in the September 18, 1952 issue of *Tri-County News*.

During that period of time, the well-known Blalocks were mining the Carson Rock on South Toe. It was producing a high

Yates Bennett poses with mica in a Tri-County News *photo of books found at Isom Mine. One block weighed 1,456 pounds.*

volume of larger-than-normal books of mica. The Blalocks later sold the mineral rights to Corbin Robinson.

By November 1952, the loans made to miners for the purpose of mica development were showing results. Mines, such as Macon Mines, were delivering large quantities of extra-high-grade to the depot. The combined minerals shipped from Spruce Pine in 1952 had an estimated value of $8,000,000. Feldspar led with an estimated value of $3,000,000.

Beryl is the primary ore of the metal beryllium. It was critical to our national defense and listed as a Strategic Mineral. During that period, the government wanted some local beryl for testing. Well-known mineral collector Liston B. Greene of Spruce Pine, delivered two tons for that purpose. Also, two carloads of beryl-rich rock were shipped in from North Dakota for the purpose of testing flotation separation efficiency of that mineral. I have found no record of the results.

During the 1940s and 1950s, Spruce Pine was the miners-supply capital of the United States. Even large mining centers such as Denver, Colorado depended on Spruce Pine for mining equipment. Miners from other areas who needed equipment or repair parts had to order and wait. In Spruce Pine, almost everything that was needed could be found on the shelf. Well-known Mitchell Distributors was the major supplier of pneumatic and earth-moving equipment.

Powder Man

The powder man, like most miners, would do whatever needed to be done, including drilling the holes. His primary job was to load and shoot the holes, using whatever explosive was popular at the time.

If you had been the powder man for Carolina Minerals during the war, this is what would have been expected of you: After the drill operators had completed drilling about 180 holes comprising twenty sets, you would go to work loading up to forty pounds of DuPont special gelatin dynamite of sixty percent strength into the holes. The dynamite would be armed with millisecond detonating caps providing eight delays. You would hope that this would give good fragmentation of the feldspar and leave it crisscrossed with fissures.

Blasting feldspar down was actually simple and predictable for the powder man. He was doing the same thing day after day with the same mineral, usually in an open pit. In a mica mine, underground, his job was much more demanding and the results were less predictable.

The rock alongside the mica-bearing vein was normally a schist or gneiss. This group of minerals has no cleavage, varies drastically in hardness and is normally much softer than the quartz containing the mica. Other minerals contained in the schist can cause breaking problems. For instance, the horizontal tunnel of the Isom contained thirty percent kyanite; with a mineral of this type, blowouts are not uncommon and nice, smooth floors and walls are difficult to obtain.

When blasting a tunnel or shaft, it was desirable to leave smooth, unbroken walls to prevent falling rock and have a reasonably flat floor. The vein had to be broken into small enough pieces so that the mica could be removed but not destroyed. This required even more skill in the early years, when black powder was used. Black powder was difficult to predict, and coupled with the fact that only large mica would sell, you can see that a powder man was not just anyone who could light a fuse.

Luther Thomas

On April 3, 1993, I visited Luther Thomas at his mineral and craft shop located on Cane Branch near Micaville. Due to Luther's vast amount of knowledge about local mining and minerals, it was a must that I talk to him. Not only is Luther a retired miner, but he has stayed in touch with current events that have affected the industry.

Luther came from a family of miners. Some of his brothers also followed the trade. Luther and his brothers were known by fellow miners and friends as "the five bears." I asked Luther about that, about all I got for an answer was a grunt and a grin. I am not sure by whom or why they were given that name. Other miners think it was because of their determination and dedication. No doubt they were good at what they did.

I was supposed to meet Luther at his place around 10 a.m. but I arrived a half-hour early. I found Luther in his workshop building a fire. The temperature the night before had dropped into the low 20s. The large quantity of minerals stored there keeps the temperature from rising. While I was there, I do not believe it ever got out of the 20s. I could hear the fire crackling but I could not feel any heat.

When Luther retired from mining, he gathered together some of his best mineral finds and displayed them for the public to see. This was the beginning of a second career. Over the years, he has collected the most impressive private collection of gem and rare minerals I know of anywhere. Most are from Western North Carolina. He has a museum and a shop where items are for sale.

While talking to Luther, I formed the opinion that even though he was a miner by necessity, he had always been a rock hound at heart.

Luther had worked with my dad, grandfather and uncles during his mining career. One of the first things Luther told me was about visiting an old mine on the head of Bolens Creek in Yancey County. My grandfather Cas had told him about it and had called it the old copper mine. This caused my hair to stand up a little. I had been hoping to find information about the Pensacola Copper Mining Company, especially about the location of any mine or processing plant they might have worked or used.

Grandpa lived close to this old mine around the turn of the century. I had heard him talk about the old copper mine, but had forgotten until now. Could this be one of the Pensacola Copper Company works? Some believe the old mine was worked by Spaniards or Indians.

When Luther visited the mine, the dump was covered with rock that would turn your fingers red if you touched the rock. He thinks the Indians mined the minerals to manufacture paint. I suppose we will never know for sure, but some day I hope to visit the mine before it disappears completely to see if I can determine what tools were used.

Luther's father, Robert (Bob) Thomas, was a Yancey County miner. At the age of seventeen, he discovered a mica mine that produced a lot of high-quality mica over the years. The mine was named the Charles Robinson.

Luther remembers one book of mica from the mine that weighed about 200 pounds. It was a perfect square. When looked at from the side, you could see at least two inches down into the mica.

When Luther got big enough to carry a shovel, he would follow his father on prospecting trips into the mountains. This was how he got started on a life-long career. He got his first paying public job at the age of thirteen, driving steel for the Silvers brothers. He worked at the Bowditch Feldspar Mine, located at the head of Cane Branch, where he now lives. He used an eight-pound hammer all day.

The spar was blasted down and moved from there to the dump

area. There it was hand cobbed, loaded onto wagons and hauled to the crushing plant, which stood where Luther's house now stands. Some of the concrete foundation is still there. After grinding, it would be loaded on the Black Mountain rail cars to be shipped to the customers.

The crushing plant where Luther's house is now was the first in Micaville; two others were to come later. Over the years, Luther mined and sold mica that sold for more than $70 a pound. Most sold for punch or scrap. Punch brought about three cents a pound.

In the early days of Luther's mining career, there were very few power drills. Some of the larger mining operations used steam-powered drills, but that was an exception.

He and John Blevins worked the Silvers Mine for a while. The mica there was large and plentiful, but at the time, the quality just was not there. It looked as if this might not change. Luther moved on.

Shortly after that, he and Charlie McCurry worked the Willie Shanty. From this mine they removed a lot of high-quality mica. The price for good mica was excellent.

My Uncle Herman lived on Bolens Creek at the time and he always kept a good team of horses. Whenever Luther was mining near there, he would hire Herman to haul his mica out.

Luther remembers drilling overhead using a jackhammer and not having a jack's leg to use. A jack's leg is a metal apparatus used to hold the heavy hammer overhead and could be adjusted as the hole was drilled. When drilling overhead by hand, not only did you have to hold this bouncing heavy chunk of iron up, you had to maintain enough pressure for the steel to cut, not to mention all the debris falling all over you. I personally could not think of a more painful way to destroy your body. Drilling deep holes overhead by hand could be just as, if not more, painful. The shaker would hold the heavy steel against the rock while the driver would have to swing up. After a set of deep holes was drilled, your body would have to ache.

Luther worked a lot with his grandfather, Charlie McCurry. Charlie was an old timer with ways to match. I am sure this sounds familiar to many. Rain or shine, summer or winter, get-up time was 4 a.m. The fact that you were going to be at the job site an hour before daylight did not make any difference.

Luther says the prettiest mica he ever mined came from Gouges Creek in Mitchell County. Pete and Zeke Carrol owned the lease and had been mining for feldspar but temporarily were at another location. Luther asked and got permission to go ahead and work the mine for mica.

He had been at this location before and from all the mica left lying around, he figured it would be worth the effort. The mica was not located in the spar but alongside a vein of flint that went up the hill away from the spar. The first day he took home 225 pounds and hid another 100 pounds or so that he could not carry. Someone borrowed that 100 pounds, or at least it was not there the next day. For the 225 pounds he took home, he got more than $600.

The mica was a uniform green color, exceptionally high quality with very little scrap. Luther showed me a couple of pieces which he still has. I agreed that this was beautiful mica. I had never seen mica that would ring like glass when bumped. Unfortunately, the deposit was small. He says the Green Mountain Mine and the Stanley both had a beautiful rum-red mica.

One time Luther, his cousin Guy McCurry, and Charlo (Charlie) Hyatt were working the Green Mountain Mica Mine. Luther and Guy were cleaning out the muck; Charlie was on the jackhammer drilling another round of holes. A couple of small pebbles fell, striking Luther on the back. This caused him to look up. What he saw must have been an eye opener. A boulder weighing several hundred pounds had broken loose and was falling straight down on Guy and himself. Charlie was off to the side. Luther screamed and jumped to one side hugging the wall. Out of the corner of his eye he saw two flashes. Guy jumped at the same instant the huge boulder hit the floor. The boulder shattered like an exploding bomb. There were several minor injuries. A hand-sized chunk struck Charlie on the forehead. The bleeding was heavy but the round of holes were almost complete, so Charlie stayed with the job until they were finished. Apparently, freezing and thawing close to the entrance had caused the near disaster.

He had another close call at a mine on Cane Branch, where he was working for scrap mica. Luther was down in the mine loading rock in the muck bucket. When full, the bucket was lifted out by a mule-powered hoist. All day he had been uneasy; something just was not right. Most of the time while the bucket was being emptied, the mucker would go about other chores. This day, Luther would stand to the side and watch the bucket being lifted out and back. Sure enough, just as the bucket reached the top, the cable broke and came crashing back to the bottom. Luckily, no one was hurt.

Even though scrap mica did not sell for a high price, the books of mica from this mine were so large and plentiful the mine could be worked profitably.

During one period, Luther cut and graded mica for the government. That lasted for about three years. At one time he also worked his own crew, grading and sheeting mica. He said some of the books of mica from the Cattail (Isom) Mine were so large they were turned up on edge and worked on the floor.

Luther spent about forty years working in the mining industry. One thing he said he would do differently was to save more of the minerals that were mined. Luther followed suit with most miners at the time. Whenever a unique mineral specimen was found, it was marveled over, maybe even kept for a while, but eventually would be discarded. More than likely, it would not be picked up or given a second thought. Many beautiful gemstones have been ground up and discarded as waste.

Luther's son Ira has a mineral shop at Spruce Pine and has the Grant Floyd, Roby Buchanan and Floyd Wilson Collections in his possession. All these people were well-known Western North Carolina mineral collectors and lapidarists. His other son, Ickett, has a mineral shop close to the South Toe River Elementary School in Yancey County.

In the mid-'40s, Luther cut and graded mica from the Presnell Mine. Tommy Thomas, Luther's brother, supervised a crew at the mine. Luther also kept the books and worked the mine when he had spare time. Luther employed several people to grade the mica.

At one time a mining company from Pennsylvania with interest in mica decided to open the Presnell ,which had been closed for several years. The mine was one vertical shaft high on the ridge above the South Toe River. The plan was to start a horizontal shaft about one hundred feet above the river, go straight back for eighty feet, a slight decline for eighty feet, and straight back until they came to the pegmatites. This course should bring them under the old vertical shaft a safe distance. The old shaft was full of water, so the engineers could not get an accurate depth measurement. Luther had worked this mine before and knew it was deeper than the engineers figured. They came out in the bottom of the old shaft.

All the water and debris poured into the new works. It took about two weeks to pump the water out. Next came the clean up of trash that poured in. While cleaning up the trash, Luther had several foot races with boulders that would turn loose from the walls of the old shaft. They turned loose and bounced from wall to wall on the way down. The noise was awesome. When Luther would hear them start, he would drop everything and run back into the new works and wait.

From that intersection, the vein went down at a steep angle for about one hundred feet, made a turn and went another one hundred feet. The grade was steep, but tracks were laid and a muck car was used.

One day Luther was working on top, dumping the muck car. Tommy was operating the hoist. James Tipton and a fellow named Laws were working inside. Sometimes, as the muck car made the sharp turn or knuckled over, it would jump the track. James Tipton was following the car out just in case it did. The loaded car made the bend okay but just as it started to knuckle over, the cable broke. James made the snap decision to try and outrun the car to the turn, where it would probably jump the track. It did derail but at about the same time it caught him. He was fortunate. The other minehands came to the rescue and got him out from under the load of rock. He had some serious wounds but healed over time.

The Presnell Mine never did quit producing mica but the quality dropped until it was not worth mining. Later, test holes were drilled that found other veins of mica but those were never mined.

Luther talked about the Shanty Mine. It was the only left-handed mine he ever worked. That threw me a little. I knew they came in all shapes but I did not know they came left or right handed. He explained that the slate laid to the right and the opening had a tendency to lay that way. As you entered the mine, you had a tendency to walk with your left slightly to the front. This kept your face from being so close to the wall.

He said the vein in that mine was exceptionally narrow. The mica was not found in the vein but was alongside in the slate. The last time he was in this mine you could see the holes in the slate where large books of mica had been removed. When the vein got wide where you would expect to find mica, there would not be any but when the vein narrowed to almost nothing, there would be plenty.

When Luther left mining, he went to work for an electrical power company in Virginia. After a while, he opened his own mineral museum and craft shop at Micaville. Before I left, Luther showed me some of his fabulous collection; it was great.

Kelse Boone

C ould you imagine the look on someone's face today if you told them you needed a bucket made of quarter-inch thick steel plate that would hold two tons of rock or two yards of dirt? This bucket would also need a bail constructed in such a way that one person could dump the load.

Old-timers might have to mine the magnetite to manufacture the iron needed to make the bucket. If they did not, the job would go to someone else because it would take weeks, possibly months, to get a wagonload of steel. They did not have a telephone. They did not have torches for cutting the steel or breakers or benders. They did not have welding machines. They did not have electricity. In fact, they had never even heard of a trade school. If you should ask someone to do this for you today, under those same conditions, the puzzled look on their faces might turn to laughter. Of course, there are some people around today that could build the bucket for you under those conditions. During the early days of mining, this was commonplace. Huge foundries were built in places like Pittsburgh to supply the metal, but the rest was up to the miners.

Long before modern machinery became available, blacksmiths such as Kelse Boone of Burnsville were kept busy building and repairing farm and mining machinery. Every town had at least one of these talented people. What their fathers had not taught them they learned by trial and error. Mr. Boone's shop was a little south of Burnsville on the Pensacola Road. The tools Mr. Boone worked with were not compatible with today's modern welding shop. Some pieces of equipment you would expect to see in a modern welding shop are: lathes, instruments that can be used to measure in precise increments, equipment to lift and move heavy loads, weld-testing and inspecting equipment, oxyacetylene, AC/DC, inert gas and possibly resistance welders, as well as sheers and brakes for cutting and bending metal, post-heating furnaces to be used on special metals, sandblasters and power tools such as drill motors, saws, nibblers, perhaps hardness testers, automatic welders and cutters. The people working there probably did not learn from their fathers but were trained in school.

If you could go back in time a few years and look at a manufacture repair shop, you would not see very much of the equipment mentioned above. First of all, good steel was hard to find and good or bad, no scrap was discarded. Perhaps the most noticeable thing in the shop was the forge. Close to the forge would be coal for fuel, a bucket of water for tempering the steel and a hammer, tongs and anvil. The floor was probably dirt. I know this sounds simple but it was not. Those people were in the business of providing what we needed and they were good at it. North Carolina miners could not have provided the minerals we needed without the blacksmiths.

I know very little about the trade but I will try and describe a small repair job Kelse did for a miner. In the late 1940s, my father, Lonnie, a fellow named Wyatt and partner Fred Hyatt were working a small open-pit mine on Banks Creek. It was summer and there was not any school so Dad let me go with him that day. During the day, someone broke the end off the pick. Today the pick would be thrown away, but not then. It could be repaired much cheaper than a new one would cost and Kelse Boone could make it better than new. When we left in the afternoon, we took it with us, stopped at Kelse's shop and showed him the broken tool. He did a little grinding with his foot-powered grinder. Next he placed the parts in the furnace and began using the bellows to pump air through the smoldering embers. Soon, everything was almost white-hot. Using tongs, he removed the tool and placed it on his anvil, paying particular attention to the position. Holding it in place with his tongs, he began to strike the tool. Sparks would go in all directions. He called those "fire flies" and cautioned me that they did bite. I do not remember if he added any metal or not but he could have. By striking the white-hot metal, he was fusing or welding it together. That was the way it was done in those days. The metal was almost hot enough to melt. He continued to strike the metal until he was sure it had bonded, all the air bubbles were out and it was sized properly. The heating had removed the temper, so after welding it had to be retempered. That was what the tub of water was used for. Soon we were on our way home with our good-as-new pick, which had cost very little to repair. That was a really small minor job but Kelse handled much larger ones as well.

As time has gone by, demands have become greater and those people that could do everything have been replaced by specialty people, like electricians, machinists, welders and mechanics who only repair a specific machine or part. On large jobs, consultants consult consultants who consult the engineer who consults the draftsman's consultant as to what machinery is needed and how it should be constructed. We do need those people now and could not do without them, but we did not need them in earlier years.

I remember Dad and my oldest brother, Haston, working the Willie Shanty Mine for a short period. This mine is located at the head of the Willie Shanty Creek, which is one prong of Bolens Creek in Yancey County. Dad and Haston carried a forge in and set it up. This was used in the process of sharpening their steel. There were no roads close by so when they needed their steel (drill bits) sharpened, it was necessary to carry them out every day.

This forge was a large table with a hole in the bottom and a pipe connected there. A hand operated fan was connected to the pipe. Dad would start a fire with wood and when it got hot, change over to coal. Haston turned the fan while Dad held the steel over the fire until it was almost white hot. Then Dad would lay the hot end on an anvil and beat it with a hammer, heating as needed until the desired sharpness was obtained.

After heating, the steel would be too soft, so it would have to be tempered. Dad would do this by placing the red-hot end into a bucket of cold water until it turned dark, then remove it until the heat within once again turned the end red. He might repeat the process or just go ahead and cool it completely. If the cutting edge was not tempered enough, it would dull extremely easily; if tempered too much, it would be brittle and shatter.

They did not have a jackhammer at this location. All steel was driven by hand. When a new hole was started, a short bit was used. As the hole got deeper, longer bits were used until the desired depth was obtained. On location, you would find two wooden sticks which played an important role. One was called a swamp stick, with one end beaten to a pulp. If water got in a hole and had to be removed, this was the one that was used. The other stick was called a tamping rod.

One of two types of caps was placed in the first stick of dynamite. They used either electrical or fuse caps. The fuse used would burn under water or at least was supposed to. If several holes were to be pulled and a delay action was desired, the proper cap was chosen. The dynamite cover was split and lowered into the hole. The tamping rod was used to press the dynamite as flat as possible, to fill any open space. A wooden tamping stick was always used, never a steel rod. A steel rod would have exploded the dynamite. I have long forgotten their names, but I have heard Dad talk about two of his friends who made this mistake.

Additional sticks of dynamite would be pushed in and tamped as needed. The powder man would determine how many were needed—too much and the mica would be destroyed, not enough and it would have to be shot again.

The top of the hole would be filled with sand. A hole that did not explode was a miner's worst nightmare. Someone had to go back into the mine, not knowing when the dynamite might explode. All the material placed on top had to be removed by hand and another cap set in place. This was time-consuming and dangerous.

Before dynamite became available, black powder was used. The amount of power produced was hard to predict. If wet, it would not explode and it was expensive. Nitroglycerin was used to a lesser degree. I have never heard of heat and cold water being used to break rocks in a mine, but it was used some when Western North Carolina railroads were being built.

I was small when Dad and Haston were mining the Shanty, but I do remember playing with that big red wheelbarrow while they sharpened steel. They did not stay there long. Haston went into the Army and Dad pulled the curtains on this mine, then went on to another one.

Talmadge McMahan

O n May 24, 1993, while traveling through Celo, I spotted Talmadge McMahan and his wife, Maggie, on the front porch of their home. I knew Tab, nicknamed Tab Mac, was a retired miner and I had been looking for an opportunity to ask him some questions on the subject. Tab and Maggie are good, honest people and a pleasure to talk with. Tab is extremely knowledgeable about mines, miners, minerals and the mining methods used during the first half of the twentieth century in this area. The great part is, he does not mind talking about it.

One of the hard-rock mica mines that Tab worked was the Myra Gibbs. I had rock-hounded some in this old dump and was familiar with the location, on the west side of Grindstaff Road just east of Celo off Lower Browns Creek. The entrance to the mine is a vertical shaft for seventy-five feet; at the bottom of that is a horizontal shaft going east and west. At first, float mica was found on top of the ground, probably put there by an underground stream flowing to the surface. The mica trail was followed to its source, which was a large pegmatite. The pegmatite was at a depth of about 75 feet going from west to east on a slight decline.

The pegmatite was mined to the east first. The mica was large crystals of red-rum muscovite. A wench was used to pull the track-guided muck car to the vertical shaft, where it was dumped into a large bucket and hoisted to the dump. This shaft was worked to a point under South Toe River, if not beyond. The best I remember, it probably is between five and seven hundred feet to South Toe. The distance became so great, they decided to sink another shaft into the deposit closer to the river. To correct this, plans were made to sink a vertical shaft as close to the river as possible. The new shaft would connect with the horizontal shaft. From there, they could work the mine under the river. An expensive bridge would not be needed. The mine shaft had been on a gradual incline, so the new shaft would cost a lot of money because of the depth. First they decided to mine the deposit to the west and see if there was any mica there.

Tab McMahan shows off the car he purchased with the wages he earned working at the jig mine.

They would go for ten to fifteen feet without a trace of mica and then the mica concentration would be extremely heavy. This pattern continued throughout.

One day they drilled a set of holes and pulled a shot. Lo and behold, they had drilled a hole dead center in a book of mica larger than the muck bucket. The blast had damaged the book, but it still could be salvaged. Before the blast, it was estimated to be a little over four feet in diameter.

This happened during the Colonial Mica Company days. Tab worked this mine with Floyd Chrisawn and others for a long period of time. When the bottom fell out of the price, the mica was still plentiful but they were forced to close the mine. Before it filled with water, Tab went back in and removed the muck car track and other machinery. The shaft to the east was never mined again. The deposit to the west was still producing when mining was stopped.

Tab talked about another mine he and Corbin Robinson worked near the top of Celo Knob. The shaft of the mine went into the side of the mountain at a steep decline. He could not recall the mine's name. The mica was not large but it was of extremely high grade. I believe from the description it was the Bill Autrey Mine. This mine had a cook and bunkhouse. The miners would go in on Sunday afternoon and stay until Friday afternoon.

Tab went to work there with Corbin Robinson for a while. The mica from this mine was large rum red of extremely high quality. The mine did not have a road for vehicles. The miners could drive partway but they had to walk in from the Ailers Creek Road. Everything needed had to be carried in by hand. The mica had to be carried out or hauled out by horse and sled.

John Carroll, a local miner, was working the Myra Gibbs prior to the time Tab worked it. Tab said there was a mica-grading house where his house now sits. This was the mica grading house John Carroll used. In the beginning, the building had been a grist mill that Charles Bryant operated for many years. The local grist mill had become obsolete, so this building was used by the mica industry. After the mica industry left the building, Tab remodeled and used it for his home.

Tab said he and Floyd Chrisawn got tons of mica from the Myra Gibbs and it showed no signs of depletion when it closed.

Tab also worked the Moody Rock Mine on Mile Creek in Yancey County. One time Tab pulled a shot there that ripped one of the ladders loose from the wall except for one nail. Tab did not find this out until he was on the ladder, fifty feet from the bottom of the mine. The ladder began to swing back and forth. He was lucky that it did not loosen completely before he reached the bottom.

Maggie, Tab's wife, used to gather galax for the floral industry, as have many people in the South Toe area. One day while doing this high on the mountain above the Ailers Creek next to the Lindsey Mine, she discovered a pocket of mica. At first she saw an exceptionally large book of mica float sticking from the ground. Float is a mineral that has moved away from where it was formed. She removed this book. Behind that was more. She started removing dirt by hand. The more she moved, the larger and more numerous the books became. She covered the site and could not wait to get home to tell Tab. Before they had a chance to explore the site, the word got out but no one knew the location. People in the business tried to pay her to tell them the location. That was going to be her and Tab's mine. She was not about to tell them the location.

One day it was snowing and the weather was bad in general. The jig mine where Tab worked was going to be closed that day. Maggie saw her chance and woke Tab early. They headed to the prospect. Maggie knew the forest well and finding the location was no problem. Tab noticed the dirt was soft, with few rocks, but could not argue. There was a pile of mica there. That turned out to be the problem there was only a pile; apparently a miner had hidden the mica he had mined from the Lindsey for some reason. This was the only mine Maggie did—or, more appropriately, did not—find.

Tab spent most of his mining years working at the jig mine on Lower Browns Creek at Celo. Minerals from a jig mine were removed from the ground using water under pressure.

Most families were large and had to be provided for; this took cash. Industry in Western North Carolina's rural counties mostly consisted of farming, lumber and mining. Some of the counties also had galax and that industry was much larger than one might think.

Tab chose mining and Maggie chose galax. After leaving the jig mine, Tab went to work for Diamond Mica mining sheet mica. The sheet-mica industry paid better, but most of the work was underground. Most of the scrap-mica mining was open-pit. In 1997, Tab and Maggie are still healthy and live at Celo in Yancey County.

Family Stories

My father, Lonnie Presnell, was a professional miner and primarily worked in mica mines. When he got home from work and started to empty his pockets to clean up, he would reach into the bib pocket of his work clothes and take out a handful of aquamarine crystals. During the day, he just could not resist picking up the best ones and putting them in his pocket. He had a big metal can in which he kept the extra nice ones. There he kept the best of the best, and the other ones were put wherever. Over the years, they were either discarded or lost.

One evening during this ritual, he pulled out a large watermelon-colored tourmaline crystal he had found. Since rock hounding has become my primary hobby, I have wondered just where he found it. At the time, he was working at the Bailey works at the Ray Mines. Dad gave the metal container to my oldest brother Haston, who apparently did not know the significance of the crystals, so no particular care was taken of them. The can was lost while he was in the military during a transfer to Germany.

Most of the mica mines were so far away from decent roads the miners would build a bunkhouse and kitchen. They would spend the week on location, coming home on weekends. When Dad was working the Willie Shanty, Stanley or Balsam Mines at the upper end of Bolens Creek, lots of times Mom and all of the children would walk to the mines. We would spend the day there and sometimes the night. We would sleep in the kitchen on the floor.

While working at the Balsam, a deep vertical shaft mine, Mom would position herself where she could watch for Dad to come to the surface. After awhile, she would see the faint glow of the carbide lamp Dad was carrying. After what seemed like a long period of time, he would surface. Before electrical power became available and at operations too small to justify the cost, carbide lamps were the primary source of light. The lamp actually provided very little light but was available and dependable. The lamp itself consisted of two chambers, a reflector, valve, flame nozzle, some internal plumbing and a hook to attach it to your headgear or clothing. The bottom chamber would be filled with calcium carbide; the top one would be filled with water. A valve between the chambers could be adjusted by the user to allow enough water into the bottom chamber to produce the desired flame size. When water and calcium carbide are mixed, hydrogen and carbon are produced, known as acetylene. Acetylene has a great range of flammability, which was ideal for use by underground miners.

Normally, the air in the mines would be low on oxygen and high on moisture. The carbide lamp wasn't ideal. It produced a bad odor. The charge would only last a short while and the light wasn't very bright. The flames were extremely hot. If a large container of calcium carbide became wet, a violent explosion could occur. The flame was highly carburized, loaded with carbon, and produced a lot of soot. Other than that, it worked okay.

In vertical shaft mines, the miners would make ladders using large trees, normally balsams for their light weight. At intervals, they would construct floors which were just ledges. This would support the ladders.

When blasting, they would pull the bottom ladders up. Occasionally a blast would not perform as expected. It would destroy bottom floors along with the ladders and equipment.

The few times I went down into mines and had to climb out were experiences to remember. I was young and accustomed to work, but being in the mines made me tired. It seemed my body would get heavy as lead. Every muscle ached. Now I know why—there was very little oxygen in those mines. Some miners did not make it.

Once, my Uncle Amos, Uncle Stanley, Bassey Bennett and

Champ Silvers were working the Moody Rock Mica Mine on Three Quarter Creek in Yancey County. Stanley was the hoist operator. He lowered Bassey and Champ into the shaft in the muck bucket, then he proceeded to prepare the top side for the day's work. Meanwhile, Bassey and Champ found there was little to no oxygen in the air. They got in the bucket and rang the bell to be lifted out. Stanley had gone to the storage shed to get equipment and did not hear the signal. When they decided there wasn't going to be a response from Stanley, they started out by ladder. Champ did not make it.

Another time at the upper shaft of the Isom Mine, they were going to blast. By procedure, Dad would make a final check of electrical lines. When he was out, he would give the hoist operator the okay to pull the bottom ladder out. Dad found some problems and took longer than normal. The hoist operator got the word from someone else that Dad had cleared the mine, so he brought out the bottom ladder, which was constructed of two large balsam trees. He did not know that Dad was hanging on the bottom.

The shaft was vertical and several hundred feet deep. The ladder would flail from side to side and Dad could not get off. If he had managed to jump off on one of the floors he knew the blast was the next step. The ladder was close to the top when it became lodged. The hoist operator lowered the ladder a short distance, opened the throttle to full power and started out again. Those winches were powerful machines—powerful enough to break the ladder to pieces if care was not taken. On the next try it became lodged again. Uncle Amos saw there was a problem. He moved to a position where he could see the ladder. From there he would give hand signals and possibly save it. Amos got to a position where he could see just before the ladder was about to break. Dad was holding on for dear life. He had to know his life was close to ending. Thanks to Amos, the winch was stopped and Dad was able to jump to safety. There were some problems caused by the incident but later Dad was told the hoist operator was given wrong information. Soon, everything was back to normal. He was lucky to have made it out okay.

Dad's brother Herman also mined, but by the time I had come along, he had given it up for farming. He did about every job in the mines, including blacksmithing. His wife, Vernie, was well-known for her ability to cook. Wherever Herman worked a mine, you normally found Vernie in the cook shack. If there was any possible way, they would hire her to cook for the crew.

Here's one of the stories Herman told Wanda and me: When he was a child, probably about 1910, Grandpa Cas Presnell took him up to the Ray Mines. On the way up on the left side of the road was a large pile of beryl; he called it "barrel" as all old locals do. He said there was a good sledload. Over the years, passers-by picked it up until it was all gone. He showed us the big poplar tree at the Ray Mines where all the beryl was probably buried. He talked about how hard it was drilling by hand when you hit beryl or garnet, and about which mines had pretty-colored beryl and which had dead beryl.

Vernie was gone by this time. Wanda and I knew he must get lonesome, so when we could we would go over to his house on Gorge's Fork at Burnsville and pick him up. He must have been in his 80s at the time. One time we took him with us looking for wildflowers. He had as much fun or even more than we did. He knew Wanda and I were rock hounds so he would try to tell us where to find gemstones. He told us that one time while he was coon hunting on the head of Bolens Creek, his dog ran a coon under a large rock cliff. He was on top with no way to get around. A large spruce top was above the top of the cliff and he climbed out into the tree and down to the ground. There was a large opening under the cliff. He started back to see what the dogs had. It was hard to stand up without falling because of all the loose dead beryl crystals on the ground. He tried to tell us where the cliff was located but I just could not place it. His son, Keith, told me that he was in that area with Herman one day when he told him the story and pointed in the direction of the cliff. Keith was not interested in minerals and figured after twenty-five years, the coon was gone. He promised to take me to try to find the cliff.

Herman also told us about a cliff with a band of smoky quartz that my Dad had also told me about. Wanda and I got with Amos and he took us there. Most of the quartz that had fallen off the cliff had been picked up, but we got all we could carry. The color ranged from clear to coal black. I cut several nice stones from this batch.

Herman spent close to eighty-seven years roaming the mountains. He told us a lot but, unfortunately, I never recorded any of it. One thing he told me I do remember does not have anything to do with mining or minerals. Herman was not known for his sense of humor, but he must have had one. When he was a young boy, they lived in an old house back in the mountains. He had made a squirt gun that put out enough water to be a good fire extinguisher. He was out playing in the yard and saw the neighbor lady coming up the road. He ran behind the house and went under the floor, crawling to a point next to the front door. The lady knocked and grandma let her in. She stopped just inside. Grandma and this lady were making small talk. When she got just in the right spot over the crack on the floor Herman let her have it full force. With a loud scream both of her feet left the floor. Grandma jumped back, knowing there must be a problem but doubtful as to what. Grandma said, "What on earth is the matter with you?" The lady said, "Dear God, I think my bladder must've busted." After awhile Grandma asked if it was necessary to get a doctor. The lady said, "Well, I just do not know. I do not feel any pain. Let me rest awhile first." Herman never told Grandma and she never knew what had happened to her neighbor.

Uncle Herman told me he was working at a mine one time where the shaft was on a steep grade. A hoist was used to lower and pull out the muck car, which was on tracks. If it jumped the track, a couple of miners would lift it back on. One day it did jump the track. Herman was at the top end, lifting. A fellow worker was on the other end with his back to the car lifting. Herman said his hands slipped. He jumped the car and his legs went around the other fellow's neck. He said the ride lasted for awhile and was a good one. The other fellow thought Herman was playing around and quit his job, but he came back after a couple of days.

In the early days of mining and in small operations, they would drive steel, drilling by hand. One man would hunker down and turn the drill bit. One or two men would use large hammers to drive it. Once the proper depth and enough holes were drilled, they would place the explosives. The explosives used were whatever was available at the time, black powder, nitroglycerin and cornmeal or dynamite.

Mount Celo as seen from the Isom muck dump

When dynamite became available, blasting was much easier and cheaper. The other methods were expensive and the explosion was unpredictable. Before gasoline-powered compressors became available, the larger operations used steam operated drills. The preferred fuel was coal, but in most cases wood was used.

While mineral collecting sometimes, I have found the cement pads where the steam generator was mounted and the iron pipes which were used to transfer the steam.

Even though the pay was low around the turn of the century, normally ten cents to twenty-five cents an hour, there were enough workers to fill the need. During the lean years, it wasn't uncommon for a bystander to jump in and start trying to outwork you. That person was trying to impress the boss to the point where he would fire you and hire him. Good experienced men with the ability and who were willing could just about name their own price and were not in danger of losing their jobs.

Dad was in a partnership on one mining operation. He also supervised the mine. The partner took care of the books and mine problems. Dad was not happy with the deal, so he sold out and left. Before long, the partner offered him back his interest and a salary if he would come back. The offer was accepted.

Most miners would try to locate their own source of ore. Some succeeded; most did not. Uncle Stanley was prospecting high up and on the right side of Bolens Creek when he came upon a groundhog burrow. In the fresh dirt were some nice books of mica. He hired a crew to work this mine for him. This mine produced a beautiful, clean red mica with books as large as a folded-out newspaper. The mine has fallen in now, but in the dump one can find small red garnets, crystal-clear orthoclase and a lime-green apatite.

Just above the Stanley Mine is the Silvers Mine. The dump is covered with books of mica. Many of these books contain garnets pressed out flat as if ready to be set in a ring. I asked Amos about all the mica that was left. He said it would not separate. Mica that had a binding cleavage brought a very low price, so they left it.

In about 1954, Amos felt the mica quality at the Silvers Mine would get better, so he hired Kelse Boone, a local blacksmith, to build him a couple of muck buckets and other equipment. He got all the equipment together he needed and opened the mine. Just when he started to mine, the bottom fell out of the price. Some of the equipment is still sitting there.

One summer I stayed with my grandfather on Bolens Creek. Most of the time, I was with Amos at a mine on Fork Ridge. In early years, this had been an open pit mine. Amos felt they had not gone deep enough and had missed the pegmatite dike that would contain the mica. He set up a hoist and air compressor. As he would dig down in the red clay, he would cut logs and box the sides to prevent a cave-in. It looked to me like he was building a log house starting at the top. I did not realize at the time what a one-man show I was getting to see.

He would lower the drilling equipment into the hole, go down the hill to the compressor, start it, climb back down into the hole, drill holes, climb out, stop the compressor, get equipment out of the hole, climb down, load holes, climb out and blast. Then he would start the hoist, lower the muck bucket down, climb down, shovel muck into the bucket, climb out, start hoist, pull out bucket and dump. He continued to cut trees down, then cut them to proper length, shape, lower them into hole, climb down and position the logs. He and Lee Buchanan mined this location until it was depleted.

A few years later, my wife, Wanda, and I went back to this location. The shaft had caved in. In the dump we found some nice terminated garnets.[1]

I spent a little time with Uncle Stanley at the Flem Mine, located at Vixen. The mine entrance went into the side of the mountain for a distance and then took a ninety degree turn, straight down. Stanley was removing exposed pockets of mica and doing some exploratory blasting. The air in this mine was known to be bad, so he would not allow me to advance beyond the horizontal tunnel.

Stanley also worked the Westall Mine on South Toe during the early 1950s. The Westall Mine had been worked on and off since the turn of the century. It is a horizontal shaft mine. The first one hundred and fifty feet of dirt was timbered. The timbers have decayed and the entrance has caved in now. The mica was located in quartzite. It played out at a depth of about three hundred and fifty feet.

The Isom Mine, located on Cattail Creek in Yancey County, was the last mine Dad worked. There were two shafts. This mine was located on the west side of Celo Mountain at five thousand and five hundred feet. The bottom mine was horizontal for the first five hundred and twenty-five feet; then it took a ninety degree turn, straight down. The top mine was a vertical shaft.

During the late 1940s, electrical power was available at the mine. There was a set of tracks for the muck car. The miners blasted out a large room at the back of the horizontal shaft and set up an electric winch. The winch lowered a muck bucket to the bottom. When full, the bucket would be lifted up and dumped in the car. The tunnel had a slight grade, so the car would roll out by itself pulling a small cable and dump by itself. The winch would pull the car back and make it ready for the next load.

---

[1]Garnet is one of many minerals that form distinct flat faces when formed in the absence of impurities. The phrase "garnet terminations" refers to the end of one face and the beginning of another; the end termination is used to help identify many mineral crystals.

They had ladders and floors set up all the way to the bottom. There were large rooms that opened up like a cathedral dome. Some of the exploratory shafts had low ceilings so that you would have to be on your hands and knees. This was an extremely wet mine. Water was running and dripping everywhere. If the lights went out, unless you have experienced this, you cannot imagine how dark it could be. Absolutes are hard to reach, but this comes close to true absolute zero visibility. Not being an experienced miner, I would get a little uneasy when Dad would take me down in the mine. Dropped from far above, a small pebble or a thousand-ton slab of rock would give the same results. For some reason, I hoped if something had to fall, it would be the small pebble and not Celo Mountain with its incalculable weight.

Clarence Robinson

I met Clarence Robinson and his wife, Martha, in 1986. At that time, he told me about a few of his mining experiences. He also told my brother, Howard, and me the location of an old mica mine where we might find some nice beryl crystals.

Clarence came from a mining family and had been a miner for most of his life. On March 3, 1994, I decided to take a chance that the couple would be home and drove to the Halls Chapel area, near the South Toe River, in order to speak with them. The night before had been windy and cold and had given us a couple of inches of snow. By early afternoon the wind had subsided and the clouds had given way to beautiful sunshine. The snow was melting and it was actually nice outside when standing in the sunlight. That is where I found the Robinsons.

When I drove up to their home, I spotted them standing in a grassy spot in their backyard where the snow had melted. After a winter like we had, just being out of the house in the sunlight must have felt good. After a short greeting and explanation of my visit, they invited me into their home where we could sit, talk and be comfortable. Clarence's father, Walter B., and his grandfather, Sam Robinson, had also been miners. Over the years, Clarence had mined many different minerals at many different locations, but primarily he liked to mine sheet mica. Clarence's father, Walter B. Robinson, founded the Poll Hill Mica Mine, which proved to be one of the best producers of exceptionally high-grade mica. Sam worked the mine for several years until Burleson Mica opened the Big Poll Hill, just a few yards away. The Poll Hill was located on Blue Rock Road, on his grandfather Sam's property. Sam was working the mine for Jake Burleson of Burleson Mica when he lost his life.

One afternoon, Sam was preparing the dynamite to load a set of holes at the Big Poll Hill. The caps being used were of the fuse type and kept in a special container. Sam was sitting on a box of dynamite cutting the fuses to proper length, crimping on the cap and placing the cap in the dynamite sticks. A neighbor, Mr. Nate Wilson, an elderly gentleman, came down to talk to Sam as he often did. Nate pulled up a case of dynamite, sat down, lit his pipe and commenced to chat about things of interest. Fire from the pipe must have fallen into the cap box. The caps and all the dynamite exploded without warning. Two lives were lost at the Poll Hill that day.

Burleson Mica mined the Poll Hill for many years. R.L. Greene was mine foreman, and his brother was hired to operate the steam generator. Steam was used to operate the drills. When the boiler pressure built up to a predetermined point, a relief valve opened and allowed the excess pressure to escape. When the valve popped, the steam rushed out and made a loud noise. A considerable amount of energy was lost. Apparently, the operator was not that familiar with boilers. One morning before the boiler was fired, he disassembled the relief valve and put in another leather seal that he cut. This leather seal did not allow the valve to function. When the boiler was fired and the pressure came up, it exploded with a tremendous force. The complete boiler was torn from the concrete anchor pad and hurled into the woods where it lies rusting today. Two more lives were lost at the Poll Hill Mica Mine. Lives were never considered cheap during area mining, but many were lost. Providing the minerals the nation needed exacted a heavy cost, and sometimes it was the lives of our miners.

Clarence worked many mines during his mining years. Some of those were the Poll Hill, the Speck and the Jim Gouge Mines. The Jim Gouge and the Poll Hill, by far, produced the best grade mica of any of the mines he worked. Clarence told me something that surprised me. He worked at the Poll Hill Mine during a period when mica was sold by the cord instead of by the pound.

The Fannie Gouge Mine had the largest books and quantity of mica. There were many books of biotite mica, several feet thick, left sticking from the walls. There was not a market for sheet biotite and the quartz matrix was just too hard and tough to be economically feasible to mine for scrap. In 1926, a 4,400-pound book of mica was found in the Fannie Gouge Mine on Blue Rock Road in Yancey County. It was found at a depth of seven hundred feet and cut in patterns 28" x 36".

Before the Fannie Gouge entrance was closed, some people from Maryland showed up and tested the mine for radioactive minerals. Clarence said, "Their meters would just click and whine in certain locations." They could only check the muck dump. The mine hadn't been worked for awhile and was full of water. Pumps were installed and the water was removed. Carl Robinson was employed full-time to keep the water pumped out and watch the mine.

About once a year for several years, a crew would come in, blast down fresh material and haul it off. Clarence did not know where it was going or what it was being used for.

The Fannie Gouge was deep compared to other mica mines. The shaft heading goes to the northeast and at a grade that can be walked. Spruce Pine Mica worked the mine for many years. Well-known miner Ben Blalock was the foreman of many of the mining jobs Clarence held. Clarence liked mining for sheet mica the best.

When mining for asbestos, feldspar or clay, you knew what you were going to get if you pulled a shot.[1] With sheet mica, you never knew. Sometimes curiosity would get the best of Clarence and he would go back into the mine before the smoke cleared even though he knew a dynamite headache, caused by breathing vaporized nitroglycerin, would not be far behind.

One time at the Poll Hill, they blasted through a vein of garnet schist that was several feet thick. The garnets were blood red. The garnet was down at about two hundred feet.

The last time Clarence worked the Poll Hill, S.M. Edge was the mine foreman. Before mining could commence, the water had to be pumped out. That took about three months. Another time he was working a small mine he had found. The mine was on Seven Mile

---

[1] "Pulled a shot" means the explosive or charge was detonated.

Ridge near the Lighted Rock Mine. There were veins of red clay running through the feldspar. Found in the clay were iron-coated beryl crystals. Some were several inches long; a slight tap with a hammer and the iron coat would crack like a walnut shell.

The Big Spider and the Little Spider were located off Blue Rock Road. Both produced ruby colored mica, but it was spider-webbed with mineral inclusions. Clarence told me the mine was named by the prospector that discovered it. The prospector was looking at the base of a large cliff where he suspected mica be located. Sticking out was one large book of mica with several smaller books arranged to look like a big spider.

During my visit with Clarence and Martha, Martha brought out a box containing different mineral specimens she and Clarence had collected. One specimen was a beryl crystal Clarence had found at the mine. He had collected several but over the years they had vanished. I explained to Clarence that minerals do that. You put two beautiful beryl crystals in a box and one will disappear, of course. This is nothing new. Washing machines have eaten my socks, one at a time, for years.

Did you know halloysite was first mined in Western North Carolina in about 1913 and was mined for the aluminum sulfate content? Clarence did.

Clarence worked the jig mines along the South Toe River and the asbestos mine off Blue Rock Road and the one next to the Goug Rock. Blue Rock Road got its name from the asbestos deposits. Anthophyllite looks blue.

When Walter T. Hippey left Powhatan Mining Company, he mined the Elf Corundum Deposit in Clay County for asbestos for a short period of time. That mine is about 300 yards east of the Behur Gem Stone Mine. Most of the time it is covered by Lake Chatuge.

Clarence is worried about possible health problems caused from breathing the asbestos. Sometimes the water supply used in drilling became muddy. To prevent contamination of the asbestos until the mud settled, they drilled dry. Of course, the air was full of micro-scopic pieces of asbestos fiber. At the time, no one knew of the problems waiting forty years down the road.

To Clarence, working in scrap mica, clay, feldspar or asbestos mines was just hard work with little reward. During one period, he worked in a jig mine for Hawessett Mica Company. Hawessett produced a fine mica for the paint industry, referred to as P80, and a coarser mica for the roofing industry. Eventually, Hawessett sold their operation to Diamond Mica Company.

After leaving the mining industry, Clarence went into the ornamental shrubbery business. He still works at that business today when he isn't busy rock-hounding. He gave me more information on mining than I could possibly absorb in one sitting. I will have to go back one day.

Stories from Miners

Almost anywhere in Western North Carolina, if you get into a conversation with a native old-timer, you will find out how mining has affected his or her life. Unfortunately, time has taken most of them from us before their stories were ever told.

The following was told to me by one of those old-timers I met by chance one day while I was doing some work at the head of a large cove near Estatoe. I had completed the work I had gone there to do and was doing my best to get my vehicle down the rough, rocky road in one piece. As I bounced along, I spotted an old-timer sitting on his front porch. Up the valley from his house were several old mines. Thinking he might share some information about those mines, I stopped. The following is some of what he told me.

Fred King of Estatoe spent many of his 83-plus years mining or working in the mineral-processing industry. As a young man, he remembered the first hard cash he ever earned. To do that he would get up early and head out to an old mica mine on the South Toe at Newdale. There he would gather a sack of scrap mica. All he could carry was forty pounds. His brother worked at a grinding plant located just below where U.S. Highway 19 crosses over the South Toe today. (That operation was the Peltz Mica Company, named after its founder, Emile Peltz.) There was no bridge there, so he would wade the river at the ford. He got two and one-half cents per pound for the mica.

Fred worked for Carolina Minerals Feldspar Crushing Plant and Clay Operation in Spruce Pine for many years. There he lost most of one hand in an accident. He worked the McKinney Spar Mine for awhile. One of his jobs there was to make sure no rocks became loose or that there were loose ones left in the walls of the shaft. When checking and removing loose rocks, Fred would lower himself down the wall on a rope, swinging from side to side.

Fred worked at many mining operations before turning to carpentry work. Before I left, Fred came down to the drive where I was parked and pointed to a large beautiful home on the hill up from where his home sits. That was the last house Fred built. The meeting with Fred was by chance; I hope to get the chance again.

Most mining in Western North Carolina has stopped today due to synthetics, foreign competition and pollution. In a way, this may be good. The minerals will still be here when the world needs them and our men and women will be ready to deliver, as they have so many times in the past.

In trying to get good coverage of the miners, mines and minerals of Western North Carolina, I needed to talk to a man who had been involved with the feldspar processing industry. I asked around and was told the man I needed to talk to was James Jones of Bowditch. He had recently retired from the spar industry.

January 29, 1994 was a cold rainy day on South Toe. I figured this was a good day to try and catch Mr. Jones at home. Surely he would not be out on a day like this and might like some company, since he lived alone. I managed to locate his home with no problem. It was within a rock's throw of the old Feldspar Corporation Grinding Plant at Bowditch. Mr. Jones was at home. When I knocked on the door I heard someone call, "It's open, come on in." I knew right away this was a person I could talk to.

James is getting close to eighty years in age. He had worked about all his working years with feldspar. One of his first jobs was working as a mucker at the Dave Gibbs Spar Mine. James remembers that job being back-breaking work with little reward. His job there was to shovel muck into a waiting car.

This was during the early days of the Great Depression when very little spar was being mined. All spar had to be hand-cobbed and all waste had to be removed, including dirt. Only the best spar with absolutely no contamination could be sold.

James said, "During the Depression there weren't any paying jobs to be had. What few jobs there were in mining only paid enough to prolong starvation." James managed to stay busy at various mining locations until the New Deal provided jobs building the Blue Ridge Parkway. He was able to get one of those jobs. It paid $1 per ten-hour day. He stayed with that job for five years, working himself up into powderman position.

During the Depression years, number one spar was the only quality that would sell. As the years have gone by, the industry has shifted from number one spar to number two. James says there is no doubt there is plenty of high quality spar left to be mined, but new mines are not opening due to environmental and financial problems. If the selling price of number one spar was about $100 per ton, Western North Carolina could supply the total United States' demand. On today's market, private miners cannot sell their spar at any price.

James helped build the grinding plant at Bowditch and worked there for thirty-three years. He remembers working there the day the Soap-O-Lene Factory burned. One gasoline-powered and one electric-driven water pump were quickly put into service. The air and surface temperature was so cold that wherever the water landed, including on their clothing, it turned to ice. The soap factory was lost but the grinding plant was saved. The loss of the soap factory did not affect the Yancey economy very much.

The factory production was at the lowest ever. For many years, Wesley Robinson was the grinding plant manager. Working there also were Pete Coletta and Lee Hilliard, whom I remember as being sheet-mica miners from earlier days.

James said he worked at several small spar mines before going to the grinding plant. He worked from daylight to dark. Whenever he got a load out he would haul it to the railroad depot at Micaville. From there it would be taken to Erwin for grinding.

James said the first grinding plants built at Micaville were totally inefficient. The grinding apparatus was a large rotating drum. First, the spar had to be free of all foreign matter. This had to be done because at the time they did not have an effective method to separate the minerals. After it was cleaned, the spar was dumped into the large drum. It was rotated, causing the chunks of spar to bump into each other. Occasionally, the fine spar would be dumped and bagged for shipment. The larger chunks would be returned to the drum with fresh material and the process would be repeated. Dry grinding and pre-cleaning had at least one advantage. It did not have to be dried.

The Bowditch plant used a grinding process that was continuous. The spar was ground to customer specifications. Soap-O-Lene used spar that was a medium-coarse grind. Glass makers wanted coarse grind. After the Bowditch plant closed, James went to work at United Feldspar Corporation's Spruce Pine plant. The Spruce Pine plant used the flotation-separation method.

This was a much faster and less expensive method than hand-cobbing. This was good for the feldspar industry but bad for the amateur mineral collectors.

In earlier times, all minerals such as garnet, tourmaline, aquamarine and mica were considered waste and left on the dumps. In modern times, those minerals would be ground into a fine powder and separated. To separate, the ground minerals were placed in vats of chemicals. The heavy minerals sank to the bottom. The light minerals floated off. The minerals were then placed in a long spiral rotating heated drum for drying. This system is expensive to operate, but a huge volume of high-quality minerals can be processed in a cost effective fashion.

James remembers when clay was being mined from the Micaville quarry or Harris Clay Mine just east of Micaville. The raw alaskite was mined and loaded into a flume line. The flume line went down hill toward Micaville, turned north and followed the stream to the processing plant located at the Backus railroad siding. When the raw minerals reached the processing plant they were ground and separated. The kaolin went to china manufactures. The reclaimed mica went to other various manufacturers. The sand was used to manufacture concrete or was discarded.

The building that was built there by Harris Clay to be used for the company store is still in use.

When James mentioned the Backus siding, that caught my attention. My great-grandfather Amos had lived in that area for sixty years before the railroad came through. The Parsley brothers had told me about the Cas siding. My grandfather was named Cas and he had a brother named Backus. Were they named after these areas or the opposite? Perhaps there is no connection at all.

James worked at the Bryson City Spar Mine. It was good-quality spar but the deposit was too small to support an on-site processing plant. The spar was trucked to Spruce Pine for processing. At one time, the company he worked for purchased a large deposit in Connecticut. He did not remember the exact location but it was not far from the Connecticut River. He was asked to go up and help construct a processing plant.

The plant was constructed. Mining and processing commenced. It seems the local people were not used to this kind of hard work. Eventually, families from the Spruce Pine area were moving up to operate the mine and plant.

Core drilling had shown there was enough spar there to last a hundred years. The test was misleading. The deposit was filled with quartz and granite intrusions. The deposit was depleted in a short period of time.

James tried to think of some other miners in the area that I could talk to, but he could not remember. They had all died from silicosis or old age. James had worked all his life in crushing plants where the air was normally filled with silica particles.

He contributes his longevity to his lifetime habit of chewing tobacco. That seems to have kept his mouth moist, trapping the loose silicate particles before reaching his lungs. When I left James' house, he was sitting by the fire with a big chew of tobacco in his mouth.

Bassey Bennett

Bassey Bennett of Bolens Creek, Yancey County, mined for a living most of his working years. I visited Bassey at his home on Bolens Creek on October 28, 1992. The Bennett and Presnell families were close friends long before I was born. Talking to Bassey is like talking to a brother.

Bassey quit school and went to work in the mines while he was still a teenager. That would be a problem now, but it was not then. Children could work in mines until 1951, when a law was passed prohibiting them to do so. His first job was with Peewee Carrol, robbing abandoned mines of what spar or mica that was left. Robbing was a term used to describe miners that went in after the original miners left and removed what minerals were left.

Larger operations could not economically remove single books of mica, so after they left, a couple of individuals could go in and rob the mine and show a profit. They would take the spar to the grinding plant at Bowditch and the mica was taken to Spruce Pine.

Over the years, Bassey worked mica and spar mines from Georgia to Virginia. The next job he got was with the Kyanite Mine on Bill Allen Branch. He started as a water boy and worked his way up to jackhammer operator. His dad, John, worked there as powder man and brother, Chob (Lester), worked there as a jackhammer operator. There were normally five jackhammers working simultaneously. One day Bassey got careless and Chob came over and cautioned him to be careful. The very next day, Chob was not wearing his safety rope when his air supply line ruptured. He was knocked off the ledge. He was dead at twenty-three years of age.

The kyanite was not the nice blue variety commonly found in the area but was a dull grey, some pale blue and green. The deposit was massive. The finished product was used to line ship boilers. All of the kyanite was used by the military during this time.

The mine consisted of a horizontal shaft and two open pits. They removed the kyanite from the mine directly into the grinding plant. The mine foreman's name was Manson. When the plant closed, Mr. Manson moved to Kona and built a spar processing plant there. Bassey and Mr. Manson became close friends while working at the Kyanite Mine and stayed in touch for many years. After leaving the Kyanite Mine, he went to work at the Ray Mines.

At the time, Colonial Mica Company, located in Asheville, worked the mine. Frank Fortner was job foreman. The Bailey Works was one of the Ray Mines. They were working the horizontal shaft of the Bailey Works. When Bassey told me this, it brought back memories of a story I had heard my mom tell. When entering the horizontal shaft of the Bailey Works, first you had to descend into a vertical shaft for about one hundred feet, stop on a floor and enter the horizontal shaft from there. Dad and Uncle Stanley decided they would mine this location. Dad had mined here before so he knew this would present a small problem.

They were only going to do some exploratory blasting at first, so they needed a way to remove the muck without going to the expense of all the machinery needed. The Bailey is located on a steep ground slope.

They decided to go down the hill a short distance and blast a shaft to the vertical shaft coming in on opposite sides, the shaft Colonial had mined a few years earlier.

Mom lived close by, so lots of times she would take Dad's lunch to him. Most of the time she would find Dad and Stanley drilling holes. They eventually broke through, just where they wanted to, straight across from the horizontal shaft. The next time she delivered lunch they were in the back of the tunnel working. She could see some light coming down through the vertical shaft so she decided to go back to that point and wait. She was amazed at what she found. They had placed a plank over the shaft to walk over and roll the wheelbarrow. She could not remember how deep the shaft was from there but she could not see the bottom. She went outside and waited there.

Later the entrance to this tunnel was covered over. Very little mica was found in the horizontal shaft. Colonial kept working this shaft for the spar. The deposit was worked for several hundred feet; the shaft struck northeast and extended under the nearby stream and mountains.

In the late 1930s, sheet mica was bringing $7 a pound. Punch mica brought much less. Mica was the moneymaker but spar brought enough money to pay expenses. According to Bassey, this was a high-quality spar and never did play out.

Bassey left Colonial Mica Company and went to work for Deneen Mica Company at the Isom Mine. Uncle Herman worked there as a blacksmith at the same time and his wife, Vernie, was the cook. Walt Riddle was the hoist operator and Bassey worked in the mine. There was only a sled road to the Isom. To get there, they would walk in from Bolens Creek on Sunday and walk out on Friday.

Bob Atkins of Pensacola used a team of horses, sled and wagon to haul supplies in and mica out. Bob would use the sled the last half mile because the grade was too steep for a wagon. He would make several trips down to where he parked the wagon. When he started down, Bob would climb on top. When gravity overcame friction, the horses would sense this and go into a full gallop. It was quite a show when they crossed the stream at the bottom.

Bob had a team of large, spotted horses. In the wintertime if he got snowed in, he would fix a straw bed in the horse stable and stay there with his horses until he could get out.

Bassey said one time he drilled a set of holes at the Isom Mica Mine and blasted. When he went back in, at first he thought the shot had not pulled. While standing there trying to figure out what the problem was, he turned around and looked at the opposite wall. There it was, the shot had pulled, but the rock had not broken up. There standing against the wall was a 700-pound book of mica that looked like a mirror that had been placed there very gently.

After a couple of years at the Isom Mine, Bassey spent three years working for Uncle Sam in the United States Navy. While in the Navy, he got plenty of experience using the cleansing powder produced and sold to the Navy by the Soap-o-Lene Factory at Bowditch. The powder cleaned okay but there were no suds. This was the same factory that had used the spar Bassey had mined before. After returning home, he went to work with my Uncle Amos back at the Isom Mines.

Bassey said while Amos drilled the holes, there was not much for him to do. The mine was cold and wet. He would get so cold his bones would hurt. Apparently Amos knew Bassey was cold so the way he would warm him up was to hold him with one arm, scoop up water in his gloved hand and run it down the neck of Bassey's shirt. Bassey failed to see the humor in that but would do the same thing if given the chance.

Amos and Bassey ran the horizontal shaft of the Isom Mines. Shortly after that, Bassey went to work at the Beyers Mica Mine in Macon County. He thought all the red mineral in the mine was garnet. Years later he learned the red mineral was ruby. Bassey lives in the last house before the Ray Mines. Rock hounds would come to his house and show him the rubies they had found at Franklin in Macon County. After finding out the mine he realized that this was probably the same stuff he had thrown away many years ago.

I asked him about a mine shaft located at the head of Rocky Fork on Moody Mountain. My brother Howard and I found this old mine one day while mineral collecting. Bassey had worked this mine and it was called the Rocky Fork Mine.

When it first started, they found beautiful, large books of mica. But once they got down to rock no more was found. Later it was mined again. These people brought in a bulldozer. Likewise, they found nice books of float but the shaft produced nothing of value. Bassey also mined the Shanty Mine. He said the vein of quartz the mica was with would narrow down to a couple of inches, then open up again. When it would open up, it would have lots of mica. This was never a large mining operation but was mined at one time or another by all the local independent miners.

During the years, he mined most of the Ray Mines and has been in all of them. Three times he got in bad air. Once he was working in one of the Ray Mines that had not been worked in several years. He passed out and fell down a shaft. Luckily, the shaft was not deep. Someone saw him and was able to get him out in a hurry.

I asked Bassey if he remembered a prank that was pulled on him one time while working at the Isom Mine; he did. I was there the day it happened. The miners had a small wire going to the bottom of the mine and a bell outside. It was operated by low voltage. Bill Miller was the hoist operator. The bell was to signal him what to do. One ring down, two rings up, etc. Occasionally, the bell would start ringing and would not quit. I asked Bill what that signal meant. He said, "That is Bassey playing and I know just what to do to stop him." Bill fixed the wire so he could get it loose quickly. It was not long before Bassey started to play. Bill grabbed the wire and flashed it across a 220-volt circuit. Bassey said fire jumped off all his fingers. Fire was jumping off the wire to the walls of the mine. He still thinks all the miners conspired to get rid of him by electrocution. All the miners I talked to who had worked with Bassey agreed he was an excellent worker and companion, but you had to stay alert. He loved horseplay and pulling pranks.

When they had electricity for lights, Bassey would change blown bulbs. He would wait on some unsuspecting miners to walk below, drop the bulb and let it pop on their hardhat. I can see where this would be rough on your nervous system.

Bassey said the largest mica he saw came from the Isom. The best came from the Stanley.

When Stanley Presnell was working the mine, the price of good mica was from $3 to $7 a pound. This was in the mid-1930s. Stanley saved about a 1,000 pounds, predicting the price of mica would go up. Bassey said, "You could open the lid on the large box that it was stored in, and it looked like it was stacked full of red-tinted mirrors." Mica prices did go up, but Stanley had already sold the mica. Bassey, who has been retired for several years now, knows enough about mining to more than fill a book.

I have mentioned several trades that were needed by the mining industry but so far I have not talked about a very important one, the teamsters. Today's Teamsters are experts at driving trucks. Yesterday's teamsters were experts at driving oxen or horses. Until I was about 17 years old, I was lucky enough to live on a farm where there were always work horses, although there was farm machinery and horses were becoming obsolete. Much of the farming and logging was being done with real horse power. All the generations before me had lived during a time when there were no tractors or trucks. My grandparents were born before there were trains in the area. Without teamsters, the early minerals could not have left the mountains. Without today's Teamsters, our minerals still could not leave the mountains. There are still horses around but few people would know how to work them. Today, Teamsters know how and when to use the jake brake but how many would know why or how to J-haw or rough lock? Not many, I suspect.

As with blacksmiths, saddle and harness makers, carriage makers, handle makers, miners and muckers, cobbers and rifters, yesterday's teamsters will not be missed much. In fact, some have already forgotten they were here and how important they were.

These miners worked hard and in places that would not be allowed today, but they had high spirits and a sense of humor.

Feldspar Miners

During the last few months, I had talked to several mica miners. Now I needed to talk to some real feldspar miners. Just about everyone in Yancey County knows the Parsley brothers of Newdale: Allen, Dave, Sam and R.C., yesterday's miners and today's merchants.

On June 22, 1993, I stopped at the Newdale Grocery, their business for the past forty years. Allen and Sam operate the business; Dave and R.C. are retired. I was in luck. Sam, Dave and R. C. were there. Sam was extremely busy, but Dave agreed to share some of his knowledge and mining experience with me.

During the early 1900s, programs to tax those who would work to pay for the ones that would not work were not in existence. Everyone except the truly disabled were expected to earn their own keep. The Parsley brothers were no exception. Sam got his first paying job in the mine at the age of fourteen. Dave started earning fifteen cents an hour at the age of seventeen.

Over the years, they spent most of their time mining the McKinney Feldspar Mine, with a few years spent mining the Old Twenty Mine. In the late '40s and '50s, during the government price support program, they spent some time mining sheet mica. Rigorous quality controls placed on the mica during this period made sheet mica mining unprofitable for the Parsley brothers. The Old Twenty Mine not only had high-quality feldspar, but large, excellent quality books of mica. Carolina Minerals had the mineral rights at the time to the McKinney.

The Parsley brothers would pay Carolina Minerals for the spar they mined and then sell it back to them. I suppose the payment to Carolina Minerals went to the landowner. The mine now operates as a museum across the road from the McKinney, which was operated by the Whitehall Company. They also were operating one on the hill above the McKinney and the Chestnut Flat Mine.

Whitehall was a mining conglomerate headquartered in Connecticut with mining operations in both states. The spar that Whitehall mined here was ground to a fine powder and sold as a cleansing powder.

Dave and Sam were working the McKinney one day in the early '50s when a rock fell, striking Sam on the forehead, bringing his active mining career to an end. The injuries were massive and the doctors advised Sam to give up mining and he did. After that, he went into the retail grocery business with his dad.

The fifteen cents an hour Dave first got does not seem like much today and was not then, but it was a little better than the going rate. During those days if you found a paying job, you took it.

Dave worked for several small operations at first, but after a few years he pitched in with his brothers and started mining the McKinney Feldspar Mine in Mitchell County.

The ore was blasted out, brought to the surface by car or bucket and separated. The high-quality ore was placed on a rail car and lowered about a mile down the Crabtree Valley to the railhead. The full car being lowered would pull the empty car back. There the spar was loaded onto narrow gauge rail cars that held five tons each, ten cars to the train. The loaded cars were pulled to a rail junction with the C.C. and O. Railroad at Cass near Booneford. There, the spar was dumped into standard-size rail cars to be transported to Erwin, Tennessee for grinding.

Over the years, the Parsley brothers mined a lot of spar that was ground at the Bowditch plant. The feldspar mines of Upper Crabtree produced enough spar to keep a grinding plant busy, but one was never erected. A scrap mica grinding plant was built to process the mica from these mines. Some mica was hauled in from other mines to supply it as well.

The Parsley brothers were mining one of the many shafts of the McKinney pegmatite when, at a depth of about one hundred and thirty feet, they blasted into a vein of the rare minerals samarskite and columbite. When they went back in after the shot was pulled, they could not believe their eyes. What they expected to see was the usual white spar, but instead, there was a huge pile of shiny black mineral. Minerals from one shot sold for over $3,000.

During this period, the United States government sent a representative down from Washington to make arrangements to buy these minerals for government use. A deal was struck.

They would hear from Washington in a few days and the price would be $4 a pound, more than what they had been getting. They started to pile up the columbite and samarskite, to hold it until they heard from Washington. A year went by and no word. They put the minerals in wooden barrels, hauled them to the depot where they were weighed. Union Carbide paid cash on the spot. The very next day the government representative showed up; of course he had a good explanation, but sometimes things just get messed up.

The samarskite had a shiny surface and the columbite had a dull, weathered look. Separating the two was not a problem. They were paid much more for the columbite than the samarskite. These minerals never did play out. The last set of eighteen holes, fourteen feet deep were plugged to keep them from filling up and never pulled. Dave says the holes are probably still there. While drilling the holes the mud that came out was coal black. The holes they drilled were drilled wet. This was a smart move because quartz dust is a killer.

Dave had a large slab of samarskite laying next to an old shed. One day a fellow showed up and wanted to buy it. After Dave found out it was for the Smithsonian, he would not accept payment. As far as Dave knows, it is still there on display.

The Old Twenty was an open-pit mine. The spar was hauled to Cass on the same narrow-gauge railroad as the McKinney and Whitehall works.

Dave also worked a sheet-mica mine on the mountain at Newdale. The mine produced large books of beautiful mica, but they were contaminated with small black specks of some other mineral. This was not acceptable, so most of it went for scrap.

Dave believed mining of the McKinney pegmatite started about 1920. The McKinney was mined to a depth of only about 320 feet, but the opening was huge. Enormous amounts of minerals were removed.

In 1957, the Parsley brothers, along with partner Clyde Hollifield, sold their interest in the mine because it had become extremely dangerous to work and the quality of spar had dropped drastically. The mine closed about that time. One by one, the Parsleys all dropped out of active mining during the 1950s.

Mining corporations

Most miners did not form a corporation. Many did form partnerships but in most cases formal papers were never filed. A nod of the head or a hand shake was all that was required, and in those cases a paper trail does not exist. Corporations were officially formed, though, and the following is a list of some of those mining corporations from Avery, Mitchell and Yancey county records.[1]

• Appalachian Minerals (1937): Officers were Richard Voil, Morton K. DeBerk and Herbert O. DeBerk.

• Blue Ridge Mining Company and Celo Mining Company (1928): Officers were Pearcy Threadgill (Mr. Threadgill was a well-known land developer in Yancey County), V.R. Moffatt, Leon L. Noble and Joseph Hunter.

• Cattail Mining Corporation, (1948): Officers were G.B. Woody, G.M. Woody and G.A. Fleming.

• Pollard Kyanite (1928): Officers were J.A. Wright, J.A. Pollard and W.H. Pollard.

• Crabtree Creek Mica Company (October 27, 1898)

• Carolina Mining (1903)

• Dibbell Mineral Products (1916). It is not clear why the name Dibbell was chosen; none of the officers had that name.

• English Mica (September 23, 1908) Officers included T.A. English.

---

[1]Dates shown are dates of official corporation from county corporate records.

• In 1910, the Burlesons and Vances teamed up and formed the corporation of the Mica Belt Railroad. Their railroad was to be of standard gauge and intersect with the C.C. and O. Railroad at Altapass and extend to the Cranberry Iron Mine. I do not know if this railroad was ever completed.

• Margarite Mica (December 2, 1892)

• Iron King Milling and Mica Company (November 30, 1891)

• Penland Clay (1916)

• Linville Sand Manufacturing and Mining (1887)

• Blue Ridge Mines (April 30, 1890): Mined iron ore at Cranberry.

• Blue Ridge Mining and Manufacturing of Mitchell County (1920)

• Brown Brothers (April 22, 1898)

• Carolina Products Company (1911)

• River Mining Company (1917)

• Big Ridge Mining Company (1920)

• Burleson Mica (1901)

• Carolina China Clay (1931)

• Crabtree Mining (1898)

• Feldspar Mining and Milling (1920)

• River Sand and Gravel (1923)

• Tarheel Mica Company (December 16, 1908)

• C.J. Harris Mining Company (June 24, 1891): Officers were C.J. Harris, Theodore Harris and Joseph J. Hooker. Harris Clay changed officers and mined many locations in its hundred and twenty-five or so years of activity. C.J. Harris had been mining clay for several years when the first major organizational changes came. There must have been many things taking place during the period that could affect the clay industry. The train was about to come to Mitchell and Yancey counties, and Harris wanted to be ready. He had visited the area and knew there was a lot of clay there.

• Justice Mining (October 23, 1953 at Newland, North Carolina): Officers Robert Guy, Tyree Garland, Sam Ray and John McBee Sr. were not newcomers to the mining industry when they incorporated for a period of 99 years for the propose of mining mica, spar, clay and any other mineral of every nature and description.

• National Asbestos (June 22, 1927): Officers E.C. Guy and David T. Vance were well known in mining circles; I am not familiar with officer R. Todd.

• Powder Mill Mining (August 8, 1951): Officers were Levie Aldridge, Waits Avery and Buna Vance. The by-laws said it was legal for them to prospect, mine and buy minerals of every description and character.

• Penland Mica (August 9, 1953): Officers were J.E. Penland, M.G. Penland and E.C. Guy.

• Shaffer Mining (May 12, 1955): Officers were Levie Aldridge, John Ellis, Brook Holtsclaw, George Nesbitt and Howard Dugger.

• Southern Mining of Jonesboro, Tennessee (November 23, 1929 at Hot Springs, North Carolina): Officers were G.H. Haws, O.B. Haws and John A. Shugart. They incorporated to mine ore and operate smelters as needed. I did not find other information on this operation. They could have planned on mining copper but I suspect it was limonite iron ore.

• North Carolina Talc (August 20, 1898): Officers were Francis Hewitt, Frank Hewitt and P.A. Morgan. The office was to be located at Hewitt in Swain County. They were mining talc and marble. That mine shaft was close to the river and it closed in 1928 because the water could not be controlled.

• Tuckassegee Clay and Mica (April 9, 1914 in Bryson City): Officers were C.J. Hand and Jim Hand from Bryson City and V.H. Vessches from Holland, Michigan.

• Carolina Clay (May 23, 1906 in Bryson City): Officers were E.J. Truss, J.J. McLoskey and Thomas Cheesebourough, all of Asheville. The value of the company stock was set at fifty thousand dollars. Carolina Clay mined kaolin in Swain County.

• North Carolina Talc and Marble (August 5, 1884 in Bryson City): Officers were John Kelley of New York City, John Bradford from Maryland, John Bryant, A.M. Kelley, G.S. Bruce and D.G. Thomas of Virginia and W.S. Thomas of Waynesville. The company mined marble at Marble in Cherokee County near Andrews. They issued stock valued at $12,000.

• Swain Mining and Manufacturing (1884): The record was not clear about what they mined or manufactured.

• Great Smoky Mountain Mining Company (January 15, 1892): This was a serious mining company worth several million dollars. The legal papers of incorporation were lengthy. Some of the wording said they were allowed to dig, mine, explore for, bore, blast, tunnel, transport, carry away and sell any and all kinds of mineral substances in or upon the ground to include gold, silver and iron ores of all kinds. This also included all varieties of Carolina clays and slits, salines, gases, marbles, slates, granites and all other kinds of mineral substances whatsoever. The list of officers was long and difficult to read. Some of them were J.W. Morgan, J.W. Cline, Cyrus Hawks, Edwin A. Davis, R.E. Warnesley, R.H. Fitzhugh, Joseph Dozier, W.H. Parsons, W.T. Smith and C.B. Sevier. Most of those corporate officers were not from North Carolina but were United States citizens. Today, most large mining companies in the area are foreign owned.

Sacrifice & Changes

The mining industry of Western North Carolina has been so huge, yet almost undocumented. I have made an attempt here to leave some record to show how important this area and, most of all, its people, have been to our country. However, I realize what I have written is only a minuscule portion of the actual information. There are many questions left to be answered, with many events and experiences never recorded, known only by a diminishing few.

Our mining industry over the past forty years has gone through a major re-alignment to include minerals mined, mining methods and management. Most major industry does this over the years. At first our minerals were mined and processed by many. Most earnings were meager but they were shared by many. The people were proud of what they did even though the work was hard. Now those mines are closed and the miners are gone, most never realizing their dreams.

Many of the minerals are still being mined by large corporations. The wealth is distributed among a limited few. That is not alarming and I am sure it was expected. Some trades became obsolete and faded away. Most, such as shoemakers, clothing makers, ice providers, loggers, road makers and the list goes on, could not compete with the buying power and mass production of modern industry.

Without the sacrifice of our mining families, life in the mountains would have been much harder for all. We all prospered because they sacrificed. Let us not soon forget.

During that same period, many things were taking place. Roads went from muddy paths to gravel and from gravel to two lane hard surface and finally, multi-lane super highways. The ox and sled, widely used, were replaced by horse and wagon. The horse and wagon were replaced by cars, trucks and trains. Even machines that fly came to the mountains. Water power was replaced by steam; steam was replaced with gasoline and diesel. Coal oil lamps were replaced with electric light when electricity came to the mountains. Indoor plumbing replaced the spring house and outside toilet. The fireplace was replaced with the electric range and heat exchanger. Wooden sticks pulled by cows, used to plow the fields where the food was grown, were replaced with powerful machines.

The bed and breakfast huts located along the Buncombe Turnpike were replaced with huge motels. Everyone talks about the old-timers getting up at 4 a.m. to milk the cow. That was not it at all. They were so excited they just could not wait for day to come to see what was new.

It seems something exciting that would change peoples lives for the better was happening every day. It would take volumes to list them all. Since all this came from the minerals of the earth and so many came from Western North Carolina, it is obvious we met the challenge. What an exciting time this must have been.

Old Mines Revisted

Several years back, I was fortunate enough to look for minerals at what I think was the Andy Hall mine. The owner was reluctant to let me go there and only agreed after he found out that he and my mother had gone to the same church. The trip was worth the effort. The number of different minerals at that location was amazing. In the dunite deposit there were olivine, serpentine, asbestos, chromite and many other associated minerals. Almost at the same location was a large pile of clean vermiculite someone had mined.

Up the hill a short distance was a spar deposit that had been recently mined. A large pile of mica books had been removed and placed to the side. What appeared to have been long slender beryl crystals had been removed from the quartz matrix. Up the hill a little further was a small mine that was probably mined for asbestos. In that old dump I found some beautiful blue and honey-colored chalcedony with white lace stripes. Almost at the same location was a larger spar mine. The spar appeared to be albite. I found nothing of real interest in that dump. Within a rock's throw there was a small mica prospect where I found some small beryl crystals. The owner told me his wife had found geodes in the little stream near the house. I did not see any of those. Being a rock hound, I want to go back someday.

Different mines with the same name are not uncommon. The Balsam Mica Mine at the head of Bolens Creek was well known to me. The Balsam is located high on the east slope of the Black

Brothers on the headwaters of Colberts Creek. I had very little information about it. Up until about 1955, a local miner by the name of Nass Edge worked the mine. He would work a week at a time, only coming out on the weekends. I was at the mine a couple of times during 1955 and 1956. The equipment was in place but the mine was full of water. At that time, the area was covered with a balsam forest canopy. The forest floor was clean and the road was easy to follow. It was no more than a trail but it followed a heavy wire that the C.C.C. had placed around the wildlife refuge years before.

Wanda and I had wanted to visit the old mine for the last several years. The first visit was attempted in the mid-1980s. We had to turn back just past the Middle Creek Bald due to the downed timber and jungle of vegetation. That trip was not a total failure. We explored several prospects along the way, picking up specimens of mica, kyanite, smoky quartz and tourmaline. On August 24, 1997, Wanda and I decided to try it again. The walk is a long one and the grade is steep. The bears had broken the huckleberry bushes badly, but due to the heavy crop there was plenty for us. In fact we could pull them off the bushes by the handful. As we moved along we would pick up minerals and place them where they would not be missed on the way out. Naturally, we never picked a one of them up later. The area is still a jungle but we were determined to locate the mine. After some difficulty, we located it.

The muck car, water pump, tracks and some scaffolding were still there. The summer had been more arid than normal, leaving the mine dry. The mine appeared to be much larger than I had remembered.

The sun had already dipped below the crest of the Black Brothers. Exploring the mine and looking at all those beautiful minerals left laying on the dump 40 years ago did not leave us much time to be selective with our collecting. We filled our small collecting container with all the tourmaline, apatite, garnet, mica and beryl crystals that could be carried easily. The beryl was not that plentiful but we managed to get a couple of small crystals.

Most mineral collectors gather minerals they are familiar with, but will collect any that appear to be interesting or unusual. Most radioactive minerals fit that description. Mineral collectors should get to know something about those minerals. Normal intermittent exposure probably is safe but collecting and storing them in your house should not be practiced.

The variety of minerals found in Western North Carolina is extremely interesting to people that study minerals and the formation of minerals. Many of our minerals are found with minerals that were not formed together. You never know what you will find in the next scoop.

For those rock hounds interested in any scrap of material they can find on old mines, the following information may help:

Yancey County

• The Silly, Bitner and Vance mines were located a short distance northeast of Burnsville in the Three Quarter Creek area. The most productive mine in that area was the Moody Rock mica mine.

• From Mine Fork to Green Mountain, among many other mines, you will find the Charles Young, Laws, Hampton, Jones, Huskins #1 and #2, Deyton, Bailey and Johnson, Randolph, Letterman and the Peterson. The Peterson, located on the south bank of the North Toe River at Green Mountain, was primarily mined for spar. Bailey and Johnson was mined for muscovite mica that was said to be of a red rum color. The Gaston McDowell, Sallys Knob, Burton, Smith, Dink Rock, Red and Hilliard were located near Celo. The Fluken Ridge #1 and #2 were located near Newdale, as was the Black Jack (biotite mica was called black jack by local miners).

• The John Allen mica mine was located just over the top of Moody Mountains from Laurel Branch at Pensacola. Some of the men that worked the John Allen were Brice Ogle (my great-grandfather and Civil War veteran), John Ogle, Jack Ogle, Dave Ogle, Landon Ogle, Rollins Hensley, Charles Hensley, Jim Penland, Ford Hensley, John Hensley and Ben Ray. The John Allen mine was another good producer and was mined over a period of several years. Most of the mica was found in the topsoil. The mine was so remote, few people knew about it. I remember visiting the mine once as a child. The vertical shaft had caved in. Wanda and I tried walking to the mine a few years back. We turned back, thinking we had missed it. Later I found out we had not gone far enough.

• Several Westall mines dotted the landscape of Western North Carolina. I have written about the Westall on Colberts Creek but there was also a Westall mine located on Bee Branch Mountain. Bee Branch Mountain separates Bolens Creek from Concord. That Westall mine is due west of the Johnson Cove spar mine. Two Poll Hill mines were in Yancey County, the "little" and the "big." Both were located off Blue Rock Road.

• The Kelly Wood mine was located at Pensacola.

• The Smith, Clinchfield and Grape Hollow were located at Bowditch near the better-known Lindsey Autrey mine.

• Just north of Micaville were the Griffin, Higgins, Charles, Cedar Cliff and Bee Ridge.

• I had known of a large mine located about one mile northwest of Burnsville, North Carolina. Because of the proximity, I suspected it was part of the Pollard Clay Works. Asking around, looking for its name, minerals mined and operational statistics, I found very little history. It was worked for spar and mica. It was called the Big Spar mine but there must be another name. Sometimes the mines are so close together it is difficult to communicate as to which mine you are referring. Some of the people that had worked at the Big Spar mine were Jay Styles, Fred Davis, Audi Silvers, Landon Silvers, Ray Black, Lonnie Black, Henry Smith (who held the lease), Fred McCoury, Charles Brinkley, Charlie Gardner, Gerald Davidson, Jackie McMahan and William McMahan.

• Not far from the Big Spar mine was the Johnson Cove spar mine. At one time, Claude Boone, Chip Boone, Lat Calloway and Jay McCracken worked there. That was only a fraction of the miners who worked there over the years.

• Located on Brush Creek off Double Island Road is the Andy Hall asbestos mine. Not far from there are the Curl and the

Hughes mica mines. At Deyton Bend was the Deyton and Horse Ridge mica and spar mines.

Madison County

Many minerals were mined in Madison County but the tonnage of spar was low compared to some of the other counties. There was at least one mine that produced a lot of spar. It was the McClean spar mine, located on Holcombe Branch Road. The mine was a vertical shaft and worked to a depth of 600 feet. The spar was primarily of snow white color but there were zones of different shades of blues, greens and yellows. Some of the miners who worked there were Ralph Thompson, Lee Thompson, Rose Miller, Robert Carrol, Bert Boone and the Boone brothers of Spruce Pine. I have never visited that location but if the property has not been developed, I would like to.

Madison County was not known for its talc mines, either, but talc has been mined there. One of those mines was the Foster Creek.

Buncombe County

In Buncombe County, minerals were never mined as much as in some of its neighboring counties, but a lot of mining has taken place there.

Use of slaves to mine gold was commonplace east of the mountains. Very little slave labor was used in the mountains, if any. I was told it was used some in the Barnardsville area, but was not able to confirm that.

• High on the mountain at Barnardsville near Balsam Gap was a small mica mine worked by Yancey County miners Rollins Hensley, Richard Hensley and Garrett Harris. There are several small spar mines located along the Forest Service road leading up to the Balsam Gap through what is known as the Coleman Boundary (not to be confused with Jackson County's Balsam Gap).

• In Buncombe County, on the east side of the Black Mountains opposite Barnardsville, was the Abernathy. The Abernathy mica mine was located at Swannanoa on the North Fork Creek in the Asheville watershed. The mine was leased by Ewart Wilson of Pensacola, Yancey County. It was last worked during World War II.

• The Goldsmith Mine was located at Democrat in Buncombe County. It was mined for mica but contained numerous minerals. Mineral collectors still like to collect there.

Mitchell County

• Snow Creek was honeycombed with old mica mines. Some of those are the Persin, the Greene, the Conley, the Dave Willis, the Hall, the Sidney, the Murdock and the Phillips. In the Glen Ayre area was the Ward, Burleson and Biddix.

• Located in the Rock Creek, Lightwood and Hawk mountains of Mitchell County were the Haw Flats, Mossy Rock, Paul Buchanan, Barden, Stampy, Little Hawk, Roy Buchanan, Charles Buchanan and Burgin Rock.

• The Crabtree Basin of Mitchell and Yancey counties were mined extensively. Some of those I have written about in different sections, depending on the mineral mined. Some of those that I do not have much information on are the Wood, Cox, Gopher, Field, Chesnut Flat, Silvers Ridge, Buckeye, Carolina Minerals #3, #6, #18, #20 and #29, Harlan, Hollifield, Barnes, George Young, Wildcat, Glen and Self.

• The Self was mined for spar and was located a short distance from the emerald mine on Little Crabtree Mountain. I have never visited that mine but have been told helidor (golden beryl) crystals are not plentiful but can be found in the old mine dump.

• When traveling north on Route 19 at Chalk Mountain in Mitchell County, you can see a huge spar mine on the slope of mountain to the southeast. That mine is the Chalk and is being mined by the Feldspar Corporation. The spar mined is primarily being used to manufacture ceramics. The mica recovered is ground and sold to United States Gypsum and is used in dry wall joint putty. U.S. Gypsum has a processing facility close to the Feldspar Corporation. What you can not see as you travel the highway are all the smaller mines that have been worked in the past. A short distance southeast of the Chalk are the Childers, Black and Al Autrey.

• On the backside of the Chalk off McHone Road were two McHone mines, also the Adam and Queen. Located within the triangle formed from Rabbit Hop Road to Estatoe to Penland up the Toe River to Spruce Pine are many old mines that history has all but forgotten. Some of those mines were the Poteat, Smith, Hoppas, Drawbar, Guy, Lewis, Miller, Renfroe, Bloodworth, Griffin, Hickey, Willis and Westall. Several of those mines were served off Deer Park Road.

• The Estatoe spar mine was located just north of Route 19, at Estatoe, close to the stream.

• Most of Mitchell County mica mines produced a green tinted mica. That concerned manufacturers who used mica. To determine if the quality was affected, tests were performed. During the 1940s, the United States Geological Survey, Tennessee Valley Authority, Colonial Mica, Georgia School of Technology, North Carolina State University and Bell Laboratories tested over two thousand lots of domestic mica of all colors and varieties available. Bell used their 130AQ mica tester. Over a quarter million sheets of mica were tested. The test proved there was no relation between color and quality with the exception of biotite. Biotite was not suited for electrical use. That should have settled the matter but unfortunately it did not.

• Lenzie Ward of Hawk in Mitchell County mined mica most of his working years. Some of the mines he mined were the Hawk, Long Cut and the Birch. He also mined spar for White Hall. After Lenzie gave up mining he went into the lumber industry. Bruce Morrison and Jess McKinney were also well known miners from Mitchell County.

• In 1906, the Hoppas Mining Company was active in Mitchell County. They purchased land on Grassy Creek for mining purposes in that year.

• The Sandy Ridge mine in Stokes County had been worked for several years previously, but in 1943 it was being worked by Rierdon and Swanson. The mine was producing the best quality, quantity and size mica ever. The owners were trucking the mica to a grading house they owned at Clarissa in Mitchell County. Universal Mica was active in Mitchell County in 1921.

- New South Mining Company was mining mica on Beaver Creek in 1893.
- Zimmeral Mica Company was working a mine on Snow Creek in 1920.
- In the early 1920s, Big Ridge Mining Company was mining the English Knob mine in Mitchell County. Southern Ore leased several hundred acres on Snow Creek in 1925.
- In 1944, Mitchell County miners produced 110,892 pounds of trimmed and graded, high quality mica. Yancey County produced 290,296 pounds. Buncombe produced a little over 1,000 pounds.

Avery County

- Avery County was not formed until modern mining was going on for several years. Until 1911, official records are found in Yancey, Mitchell, Watauga, Burke or Caldwell counties. The area that Avery covers today has always produced many of the minerals that our nation has needed.
- The Mill Race was located on Sheriff Aden Wiseman's property in Mitchell County. In 1943 it was in Avery County and producing a good quality mica. Carl Meesser, Roy Arrowood and Sam Thompson were working the mine.
- The Avery Meadow, Double Head, Johnson, Elk and Landers were being worked between 1870 and 1882. The Avery Meadow produced the most poundage but the quality was poor.
- Before Carolina Kaolin mined the clay deposit located on the old Wiseman property at Ingalls, it had at least four mica mines that were productive. The Mill Race, Butler, Brush Creek and the A Number One. I believe the A Number One was one of Aden Wiseman's mines. He owned the property where it was located.
- Located on Three Mile Creek in Avery County was the Hempile. Until recently, I had never heard of that one. The Gusher Knob Road turns off Three Mile Road. The Patrick Clay Mine was last worked by Harris Clay. It is on the right side of the road close to the Gusher Knob clay mine. All the buildings and machinery that were a familiar sight for so many years on Gusher Knob have all been removed.

• The Yellow Mountains, Little Buck Hill, Buck Hill and Big Meadow areas have all been mined over and to include the olivine deposit at Frank. Most of those mines were for mica but clay and spar were also mined. One of the mines in that area was named the Honey Waits Wiseman. Waits lived at Bakersville and his real name was Waitsail. He married my great-aunt Mary Ellen.

• Also in that area were the Perth, Carpenter, Buck Hill, Big Meadow, Barrett, Pancake, Matilda Vance, Woody, Pine Branch, Benfield, Black, Little Elk, Lick Log, Bluff, A Number Two, Grapevine, Johnson, Hoppy, Fred Vance, Slippery Elm, Fall Branch, Plumtree, Emmons Hill, Field and White Rock.

• Mined just as heavily were the Cane Creek, Wolf Ridge, Spear Tops and Fire Scald mountains, located on the north side of the North Toe basin in Avery County. Some of those mines were the Aldrich, Charles Ridge, Justice, Alfred, Bug Rock, Burleson, Bad Branch, Houston Rock, Marie, Punchon Camp and the Bradley.

Other counties

• Burke County had the Bessie Hudson mica mine, among others. It was located just east of the Burke County line near Jacobs Creek. That mine reportedly produced some nice beryl crystals. The Jacobs Creek area of Burke County was not known for its mica mines but instead for gold, garnet and pottery clay.

• Jackson County had numerous mines. Some of those were the Dead Timber, Ramsey, Buchanan and Laura Allen, located on Green Creek and were being worked by Dexter Hall in 1952. All were producing large books of ruby mica.

• In 1952, the Shepherd Knob open-pit scrap mica mine, located in the Cowee section of Macon County, was also producing a high grade ruby mica. The Poll Miller Mine was located twelve miles northeast of Franklin. The Fred Cabe Mine was located two and one half miles west of Franklin.

• In 1952, the Mauney Mica Mine was being worked by the Pitt Mica Corporation. The Mauney was located fourteen miles northeast of Franklin. Texas Mining of Dallas, Texas leased several hundred acres of land located at Willis Cove in Macon County, North Carolina. At the time, Texas Mica was working the Billings Mica Mine.

• The following mines are ones I found little if any history on, other than that they were active at one time(most of the names I have listed here are in Macon County): Allman Cove, Beasley Number 1, Beasley Number 2, Big Ridge, Bowers and Cox, Cox and Davies, Engle and Cope, Frady, Keiser, Biggerstaff Branch, Poteat Number 2, Pink, Randolph,Upper Bryson, Old May, Berry, Lyle Knob, Moody, Guggenheim, Deke, Rocky Face, Sheep Mountain, Stillwell, Tilley, Turkey Nest, Thorn Mountain, Wayah Bald, Raven Cliff and Horace Thompson.

• I did find limited information on a mine located in Ashe County that was mined before the turn of the century. The Gap Creek was mined for copper and some gold, and other valuable trace minerals were recovered. Some of the information located showed the old mine was visited by people interested in mining it many years later. From the report, I suspect it was mined later but do not have information to prove it was. Someday I would like to visit that site.

Maps to Mines

Map mine locations are approximate. When planning a trip to a particular mine and the exact location is not known, there are some things you should do first.

1. Get old maps that date to when the mine was active.

2. Get current county maps.

3. Visit the area and ask natives who are friendly about the mine you wish to visit.

Many mines were called different names over the years, depending on who was working it at the time. There could be many mines in the area that you have never heard of. To help determine which one you want to locate, some background information will be helpful. Try to find out:

1. What was mined?

2. When was it mined?

3. How long was it in operation?

4. Who were some of the people who worked there?

When a mine is located that was a good producer, there probably will be many prospector pits in the area. Those are a good indicator that you are in the right location, but you might have to spend several days crossing the area to find the one you want.

Before going onto private property, get permission first. Explain your honest intentions. Do not destroy or damage any property. Do not leave any trash, even if someone else has. Do not overlook your own safety. There are many dangers when venturing into unknown areas. The author has no control over your safety or activities—you alone are responsible for that.

Guide to Map 1

01-Bud Phillips Marble
02-Banner
03-Sink Hole
04-Sol
05-Chestnut Flat
06-Emilys Knob
07-Lunday Clay
08-Jase
09-Spread Eagle
10-Pressley Spar
11-English Knob
12-McClellan
13-Riddle
14-Miller
15-Pink
16-Wiseman
17-Klondike
18-Horton
19-Deer Park
20-Buckeye
21-Presnell Mica
22-Davis Pit
23-Hawkins (active)
24-Deake
25-Bill Willis
26-Goog Rock
27-Marlin
28-Harris Clay, Micaville
29-Hoppas
30-Butler
31-Drawbar
32-McHone
33-Bloodworth
34-Estatoe
35-Fluken Ridge
36-Chalk Mountain (active)
37-Adam
38-Cox Knob
39-Black
40-W. Cox
41-Al Autrey
42-Queen
43-Wiseman Aquamarine
44-Gurley
45-Fannie Gouge
46-Chestnut Flat
47-Hoot-owl
48-Fawn Mountain
49-Big Poll Hill
50-Grape Hollow
51-Bailey
52-Field
53-Self
54-Grindstaff
55-Myra Gibbs
56-Crabtree Emerald
57-McKinney Spar
58-Woodys Ridge
59-Murphy Rock
60-Klondike Kyanite
61-Locust Ridge
62-Bill Autrey
63-Westall
64-Whitson
65-Clear Creek Mica
66-Balsam
67-Sawnee Ridge
68-George Moon Graphite
69-Rock Creek
70-Carson Rock
71-Blue Ridge Lime
72-Woodlawn
73-Charles Ridge

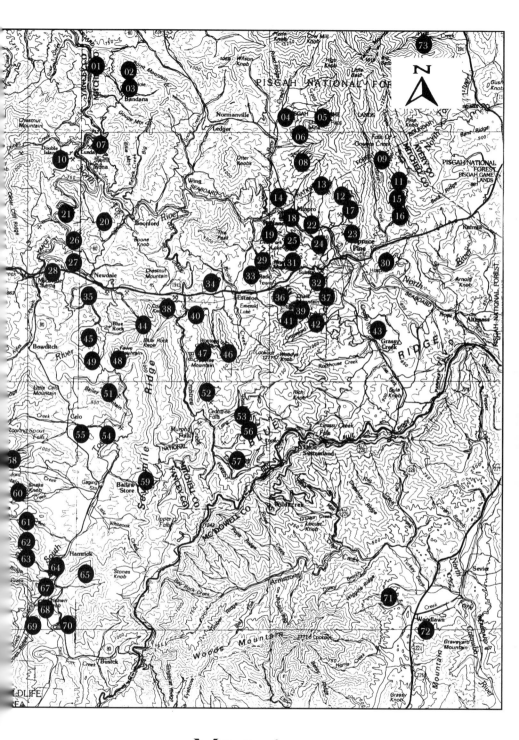

Map 1

Guide to Map 2

74-Day Brook Olivine (active)
75-Sampson Mountain Ruby
76-Moody Rock
77-Johnson Cove Spar
78-Bee Branch Mountain Westall
79-Mas Celo Kyanite
80-Ray Mines
81-Willie Shanty
82-Flem
83-Stanley
84-John Allen
85-Silvers
86-Rocky Fork
87-Cattail
88-Isom
89-Whet Stone
90-Big Butt Mica

Guide to Map 3

91-Cranberry Forge
92-Lineback
93-Elk
94-Hawshaw
95-Johnson
96-Meadow

Guide to Map 4

97-Buquro Lime One
98-Buquro Lime Two
99-Sandy Bottom and Stackhouse barite mines, consisting primarily of the Klondike, Gillesie, Betts, Rollins, Martha and Stackhouse.
100-Gahagan Barite
101-Little Pine Garnet

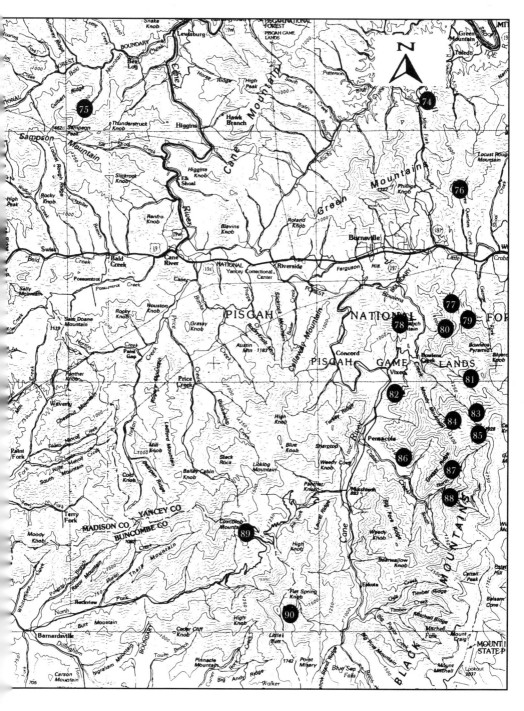

Map 2

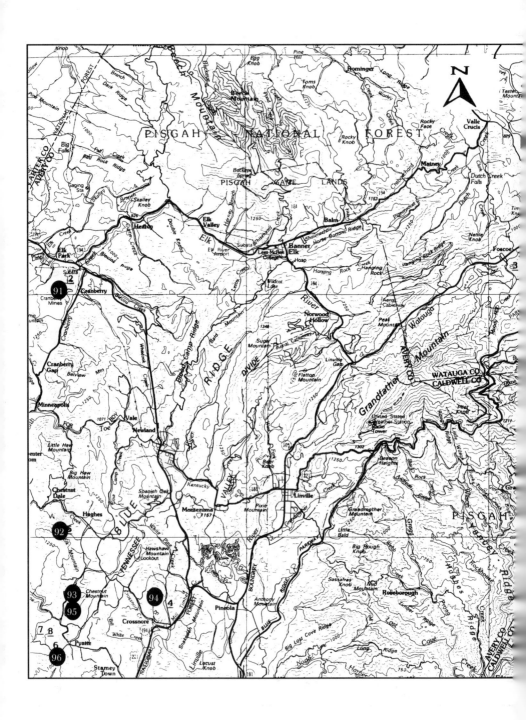

Map 3

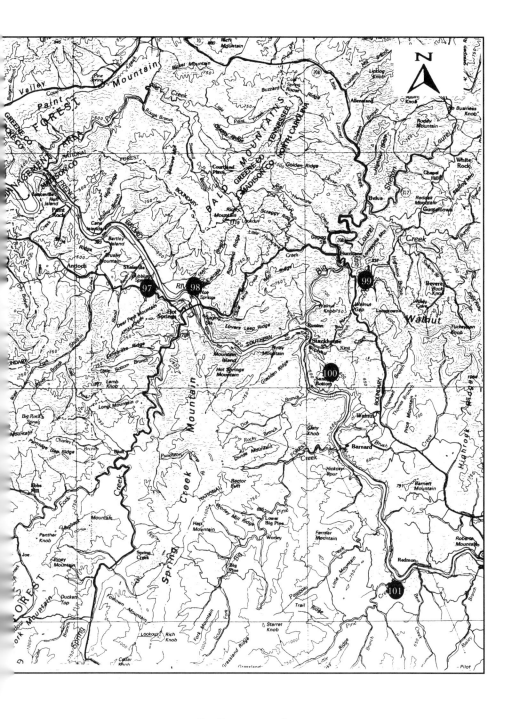

Map 4

Guide to Map 5

102-Bailey
103-Gouge
104-Ward
105-Oaks Knob
106-Punchon Camp
107-Beech Bottom
108-Burleson
109-Marie
110-Powder Mill
111-Lincoln Rock
112-Frank
113-Biddix
114-Meadow
115-Houston
116-Double Head
117-Hawk Ruby Mine
118-Landers
119-Spar
120-Happy Hill
121-Birch
122-Ray Wiseman Olivene
123-Rhone Valley
124-Haw Flats
125-Henson Creek
    Aquamarine
126-Lick Ridge
127-Mossy Rock
128-Houston Rock
129-Z. Young
130-Buchanan
131-Charlies Ridge
132-Alfred
133-Stamey
134-Beardon
135-Hawk

136-Bergen Rock
137-Clarissa
138-Horse Ridge
139-Toe Cane
140-Deaton
141-Pannel

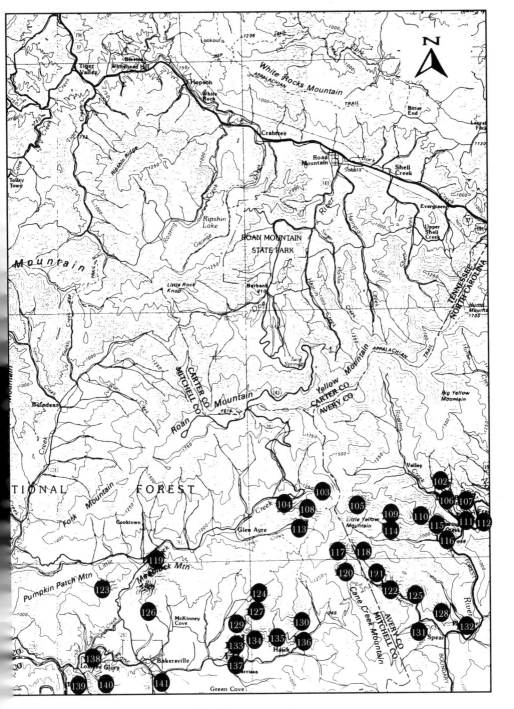

Map 5

Glossary

Aerial cable: Cable suspended from both ends. Cargo could be sent over steep, rough terrain easily.

Batch: Quality control, capacity and quantity desired determined the amount processed each batch or cycle. Sometimes called a charge, a batch number was assigned most of the time for tracking purposes.

Boiler: A large sealed container, water is placed in: the water is heated to produce steam. The steam is used for thermal energy or to produce mechanical energy.

By-product: Saleable minerals in sufficient amounts but not the primary one.

Carbide lamp: Light source fueled by calcium carbide.

Credible limit: Whenever a true story is told over and over it will be changed and at some point it will no longer be credible.

Cobbing: Breaking from host rock all unwanted minerals.

Concentration of minerals: Separation of varieties.

Concussion: Dynamite explodes from concussion but does not explode when exposed to heat. Detonator caps that provide the concussion will explode from concussion or heat.

Cord: A term usually applied to chopped wood. A cord of wood is 128 cubic feet.

Core drilling: Hollow drill rods can be used to drill to great depths and sections of rock can be placed together as removed for further study.

Cook shack: The kitchen, also could be used as cook's living quarters.

Cribbed: Unstable walls of the mine would be lined solid with lumber or logs in a manner that would support extreme weight. Cribbing was normally used where the walls of the mine were soft soil.

Customer specifications: When ordering a product the customers would specify exactly what best met their requirements and that included size, shape, weight, color and packaging.

Delayed action: If the powder man does not want all holes to explode simultaneously, electrical detonator caps or other devices can be used to provide the desired delay. If fuse type detonators are used, the fuse is cut to the desired length. Fuses are manufactured to burn at a constant speed.

Deposit: Concentration of minerals.

Dielectric strength: The ability of a mineral to restrict electron flow. Electrical insulators must have a high dielectric strength.

Driving steel: Using a hammer to strike a steel rod to drill holes.

Dry-ground mica: Mica ground and processed while dry.

Dump: Where minerals were mined and discarded.

Dynamite cap: Small cylindrical, metal-covered explosive. When placed inside the dynamite and exploded it provides the concussion that causes the dynamite to explode. Caps can be provided that are fired by electricity or by fuse. Caps are never carried in your pocket, stored or shipped with dynamite or batteries.

Electrical washers: Insulators.

Float: Minerals found in the top soil a short distance from where formed.

Floors: In vertical shaft mines floors were sometimes built to store equipment and work from. Floors also provided some protection to the miners from small falling debris.

Flotation separation: A process where a liquid heavier than the mineral to be saved is mixed in a vat. The lighter mineral will rise to the top where it can be floated off.

Flume line: Minerals such as clay could be efficiently moved from mine to factory using a flume. To use this method water and elevation are needed. A trough made of wood would be constructed from the mine down hill to the factory. Minerals placed in the trough would be washed down using gravity and water.

Froth flotation: When a mineral must be pure after separation, froth flotation separation can be used. The ore is placed in a container with a liquid that foams. The froth will leach the pure mineral and rise to the top as suds. The froth will be removed and dried, leaving a pure mineral.

Grading house: Also called mica house. A building where sheet mica was processed.

Gravity flow: Propelled by gravity.

Great Depression: The value of public-owned stock dropped drastically in 1929 and many investors lost most if not all of their money. Without investment capital, manufacturing facilities were forced to close. The Depression worsened until the mid 1930s.

Grist mill: Factory that grinds and processes grain.

Growth rings: Each year that a tree grows it leaves a ring that can be seen when cut. Information like age and annual rainfall can be determined.

Heading: Horizontal opening, direction, the beginning of.

Hoist: Mechanical device used for lifting, same as wench.

Industrial grade: Many minerals are used by the jewelry industry but most are not suited. Many of those are used by industry as abrasives.

J hold: When the teamster gave the command it was pronounced as "J HO." The command was for the horse to move to the right, swiftly, turn around and stop. The load would continue on.

Jake brake: Using diesel engine as brake.

Jib: The arm extending from hoist that would position hoist cable directly over mine opening. When muck was lifted out, the jib could be rotated over the dump.

Jig mining: Using water cannons to wash minerals from deposit. Jig mining was also called hydraulic mining.

Laid track: Railroad or muck car track construction.

Launder: A term used by the clay and scrap mica industry. A vat where minerals were washed.

Mine robbing: Removing exposed pockets of minerals after original miners are no longer working the mine.

Mine shaft: Underground tunnel associated with mining. The shaft can be horizontal or vertical.

Muck: Mine waste.

Mica book: Blocks of mica separate easily into thin sheets resembling a book.

Outcropping: Underlying rock exposed through the top soil.

Pattern: When preparing mica for market the waste was cut away. The cut must be straight from point to point and what remained was called a pattern.

Pegmatite dike: An intrusive, cross cutting, thin sheet of pegmatite minerals.

Placer deposit: Streams of water rushing down the mountainside carry material. The water slows as it reaches the bottom and the heavy minerals will sink to the floor of the stream and like minerals will concentrate. Glacial placer deposits were formed at the point where the glacier melted. Glacier placer deposits contain everything picked up on its journey.

Played out: Depleted, nothing left.

Pocket: Minerals including water and air concentrated in a small area.

Powder man: Person responsible for blasting.

Produced: Used to describe quantity or quality.

Prospect: To search for minerals. A location suspected to contain the desired mineral.

Pull a shot: Detonate the explosive.

Punch: Mica repetitiously cut to the same size and shape using a die and punch press.

Reclaimed mica: During the first years of modern clay mining, the majority of mica in the clay was too small to recover but as machinery and methods were improved, the mica could be separated and saved.

Rifter: Person that graded, sheeted, cut and prepared mica for market.

Rock hound: Recreational mineral collector.

Round of holes: When blasting, the number of holes drilled depended on the mineral being mined, host rock and quantity to be removed. The number of holes was called a set or round.

Rum colored: Brown tinted muscovite mica.

Set of holes: See Round of holes.

Sinking of steel: Drilling holes for blasting.

Spar: Feldspar.

Steam generator: Boiler. Steam generated used for power or heat.

Steel: Drill bit.

Strike: Geological term for direction.

Surface ore: Ore found in the top soil. The source could be float, decomposition of host rock or placer.

Systematic mining: In-depth study of mineral deposit conducted and plan for mining made. Mined according to plan.

Timbers: Beams or logs cut to fit and used intermittently to support mine walls and ceiling.

Yield: The percentage of the desired mineral contained in a measured unit that is recoverable.

Bibliography

Ashe County Corporate Records, Jefferson, North Carolina.

Asheville Citizen, Asheville, North Carolina, March 10, 1887.

Asheville Citizen, Asheville, North Carolina, July 30, 1942.

Asheville Democrat, Asheville, North Carolina, December 5, 1889.

Asheville News, Asheville, North Carolina, May 7, 1857.

Asheville News, Asheville, North Carolina, October 23, 1869.

Asheville Pioneer, Asheville, North Carolina, November 24, 1874.

Avery County Corporate Records, Newland, North Carolina.

Avery Historical Society, Heritage of Avery County, Newland, North Carolina.

Blackmum, Ora, *Western North Carolina, Its Mountains and Its People to 1880*, Appalachian Consortium Press, Boone, North Carolina, 1977.

Bryson, Herman J., *Mining Industry of North Carolina From 1929 to 1936*.

Bureau of Mines Publication Number 53, Raleigh, North Carolina, 1913.

Burke Historical Society, *Heritage of Burke County*, Morganton, North Carolina.

Carolina Kaolin, A Modern Industrial Romance, Spruce Pine, North Carolina, 1937.

Department of Interior Bulletin 740, 1935.

Engineering and Mining Metal Markets Report, November 1952.

Graham County Corporate Records, Robbinsville, North Carolina.

Henderson County Corporate Records, Hendersonville, North Carolina.

Lapidary Journal, San Diego, California, Published monthly.

Madison County Corporate Records, Marshall, North Carolina.

Mining Journal, February 24, 1930.

Mitchell County Corporate Records, Bakersville, North Carolina.

North Carolina Division of Mineral Resources, Bulletin 60, Raleigh, North Carolina.

North Carolina Department of Development, Economic Paper Number 34 and 64, Raleigh, North Carolina.

North Carolina Historical Review, Raleigh, North Carolina, October, 1932.

Pough, Fredrick H., *Field Guide to Rocks and Minerals*, Houghton Mifflin Company, Boston, Massachusetts, 1978.

Pit and Quarry, September 11, 1929.

Roan Mountain Republican, Bakersville, North Carolina, October 7, 1876.

Rock and Gems, Miller Publications, Ventura, California, published monthly.

Rocks and Minerals, Heldref Publications, Washington, D.C., published monthly.

Rock Products, July 1944.

Sheppard, Muriel E., *Cabins In The Laurel*, University of North Carolina Press, Chapel Hill, North Carolina, 1935.

Swain County Corporate Records, Bryson City, North Carolina.

Teacher Training Class of Burnsville, Burnsville, North Carolina, 1930.

Tri-County News, Spruce Pine, North Carolina, August 2, 1951.

Tri-County News, Spruce Pine, North Carolina, September 18, 1952.

Wilson and McKenzie, *Mineral Collecting Sites In North Carolina*, North Carolina Geological Survey, Raleigh, North Carolina, 1978.

Yancey Citizen, Burnsville, North Carolina, March 20, 1952.

Yancey Common Times, Burnsville, North Carolina, March 17, 1993.

Yancey County Corporate Records, Burnsville, North Carolina.

Zeitner, June C., "Appalachian Gem Trails," *Lapidary Journal*, San Diego, California, 1982.

Index

About the author

Lowell Presnell is a native of North Carolina and a descendant of a Western North Carolina mining family. He is a member of the Southern Appalachian Mineral Society and currently holds the office of second vice president. He has researched the mining industry for the last several years and actively pursues his interest in the field. He plans and organizes trips to historical mines and mineral deposits in Western North Carolina and has a large collection of minerals, which he shares with schoolchildren and others in the area to educate them about Western North Carolina minerals, their uses, and the history of mining.